THE INVISIBLE FILTER

HOW MENTAL MODELS SHAPE OUR LIVES

D1572447

ROHIT GUPTA

NEW DEGREE PRESS

THE INVISIBLE FILTER
How Mental Models Shape Our Lives

ISBN   979-8-88504-135-5   *Paperback*
            979-8-88504-768-5   *Kindle Ebook*
            979-8-88504-247-5   *Ebook*

THE INVISIBLE FILTER

For anyone who feels like they're stuck in a loop socially, mentally, professionally, or romantically and there's no way out.

And for my amazing mom and dad. Your support—and the patterns of thinking I had to unlearn from you—made this possible.

Contents

"Our lives are the fruit of our most consistent thought patterns."

—DR. BILLY ALSBROOKS

The Journey

It's October 1962, the height of the Cuban missile crisis, and the American Navy has spotted a suspicious Soviet submarine lurking in the Caribbean. President Kennedy has just blockaded Cuba—no sea traffic is permitted through.

Sensing the imminent threat, the sub plunges into the abyss. The Americans respond by dropping depth charges to the left and right of the vessel.

Inside, the sub rocks, shaking with each new explosion. What the Americans don't know, however, is that the vessel is armed with a tactical nuclear torpedo. And, to make matters worse, Captain Valentin Savitsky doesn't need permission to fire the weapon.

The fate of the world hung in the balance.

Let's put ourselves in the shoes of the Russian crew aboard that sub for a moment. Temperatures had climbed above 100 degrees (Krulwich 2016). And while the depth charges were meant to encourage the Soviet sub to surface, the crew was incommunicado and oblivious to the intention.

They thought they were witnessing the beginning of a third world war.

In fact, the captain even shouted, "Maybe the war has already started up there...We're gonna blast them now! We will die, but we will sink them all—we will not become the shame of the fleet" (Krulwich 2016). He then ordered the nuclear-tipped missile readied, and his second-in-command approved the order.

So, why didn't the Soviets fire the torpedo?

Looking back, it all came down to Vasili Alexandrovich Arkhipov: the man who stood in the way. When Captain Savitsky and the other senior officer prepared to fire the weapon, Arkhipov balked at the idea. He wouldn't go along. Unlike the other officers—operating under a soldier mindset rooted in defensiveness and tribalism—he argued *this was not an attack.*

Eyewitness testimony suggests Arkhipov reassured the captain that the ship was not in danger; it was being asked to surface (Krulwich 2016). Dropping depth charges left then right, noisy but always off target—those are signals, Arkhipov argued. They were saying: "We know you're there. Identify yourselves. Come up and talk. We intend no harm."

Thanks to Arkhipov's strong disapproval, the torpedo was never fired. World War III was averted.

In this example, it took *challenging the prevailing way of thinking* to prevent a major catastrophe. Which led me to wonder if this approach is something all of us can apply and learn from. What if you left a job making you unhappy to pursue what you're actually passionate about? Or got that tattoo you've always wanted but were told was a bad idea? Or embraced body positivity no matter how much you weigh?

In my own life, I've often struggled to reconcile my way of thinking with the way others do. Whether it's my unusual career choices, changing dietary preferences, or aversion to large gatherings, I have noticed an underlying pattern: people often struggle to understand perspectives that don't align with their own ways of thinking and worldviews, also known as mental models. At their core, mental models are simply the stories we tell ourselves.

While much ink has been spilled exploring mental models we can consciously activate, the focus of this book is shedding light on the stories we *unknowingly* tell ourselves which filter our thoughts and actions.

The narratives we hold about ourselves and our place in the world are the raw materials from which we build our existence. There is no greater task than shining a light on those ingredients and questioning whether they're appropriate for the recipe of our lives.

To borrow from the legendary Kurt Vonnegut, "We are what we pretend to be, so we must be very careful about what we pretend to be."

On a broader, societal level, the gap between our reality and what we pretend to be—unbiased, fulfilled, and climate concerned—has never been starker.

Thankfully, we live in an era where our unconscious biases aren't a taboo topic. The rise of the Black Lives Matter movement illustrates our society's current awakening to the systematic oppression of Black people and other marginalized communities.

But awareness doesn't seem to be equating to progress. An NPR investigation revealed police officers have fatally shot at least 135 unarmed Black men and women between 2015 and 2021 (Thompson 2021).

Why do shootings of unarmed Black men and women persist when we've never been more aware of the systemic issues underpinning them?

And despite never having more choices career-wise, we also live in a time where ennui—a feeling of listlessness and dissatisfaction arising from a lack of fulfillment or excitement—is at an all-time high.

An astounding twenty million Americans quit their jobs in the second half of 2021, in what some are calling "The Great Resignation" (Whitaker 2022). This is the highest quit rate ever recorded since the government started keeping track two decades ago (Whitaker 2022).

If we've never had more freedom to pursue jobs and lifestyles that appeal to us, why do so many of us still find ourselves stuck in and unhappy with the career paths we've dutifully followed?

Last, but certainly not least, although climate change discourse seems to be at an all-time high, we still struggle to take even the most basic steps toward addressing the problem.

That every major presidential candidate in the 2020 election had a climate change agenda illustrates how deeply woven the topic has become in the fabric of America. Nevertheless, the US still has 252 operational coal plants supplying a quarter of our electricity needs (Sönnichsen 2021; Roth 2020).

Given that The Intergovernmental Panel on Climate Change (IPCC) published irrefutable evidence that climate change is real and already wreaking havoc, why is it so difficult to mobilize a united effort to fight it?

If you're feeling confused right now, you're not alone. After diving deeper into these somewhat paradoxical issues, it took me a while to piece together what was happening. Eventually, I arrived at a hypothesis: these contradictions in our society stem from pernicious and ingrained *mental models*.

Manifesting in the systemically gross and vile treatment of Black and Brown people, pressure to pursue emotionally draining and unfulfilling jobs, and an inability to change our lifestyles in the face of imminent danger, the stories we unknowingly tell ourselves shape our lives in immeasurable ways.

I painfully realized this just the other day.

After a stressful morning of back-to-back meetings, I emerged from my condo apartment in San Francisco's Polk Gulch district feeling uplifted by the sun's warmth.

Gazing ahead about two blocks away, I became transfixed by a group of Black men talking on the sidewalk. Unlike some of the homeless Black folks I've encountered in the area, they were well dressed and appeared friendly.

Unfortunately for me, it didn't matter. Moments after noticing them, my danger radar went off, like an Allied sub detecting U-boats in World War II.

Without missing a beat, I took a sharp right turn to avoid what I felt would be an unsafe situation. I took a few steps farther before I paused to contemplate just what had happened.

As someone who strives to make their personal and professional spaces more diverse and inclusive, it really bothered me when my unconscious bias reared its ugly head.

Why did I think it wouldn't be safe to walk near them?

Would I have done that if they were White or Asian?

If dressing well didn't make a difference in my reaction, would anything?

I didn't have any answers, and it bugged the hell out of me; especially considering that I'm passionate about Environmental, Social, and Governance (ESG) topics, an advocate for unconscious bias training in my workplaces, and deeply appreciate Black culture.

But this experience made it clear that my ingrained way of thinking betrayed me. Implicit bias is a hidden mental model with frequent everyday consequences, and without knowing it, I continued associating Black men with danger.

Reflecting on that experience, I realized few of us are consciously aware of the thought patterns and worldviews subtly shaping how we think and behave. This discovery led me down a rabbit hole, prompting me to ask, "How else are mental models at play in our lives, and what should we do about them?"

The aim of this book is to explain what mental models are, illuminate their benefits and drawbacks, illustrate why understanding mental models is so important at societal and personal levels, explore how and why to apply them, and recommend ways to take control of our ingrained patterns of thinking.

As we embark on this journey of discovery together, remember that mental models are an inherently challenging topic to wrap our minds around. By their very nature, the stories we unknowingly tell ourselves invisibly influence many facets of our lives. And while uncovering and challenging our ingrained ways of thinking may not stop World War III as Arkhipov did, glory still awaits.

Those who persevere will rejoice over alignment between their unconscious and conscious selves. Solve problems better. Overcome unconscious biases. Influence others effectively. Unlearn undesirable behaviors. And live more fulfilling lives.

What's a Mental Model?

"All the secrets of the world worth knowing are hiding in plain sight."

—Robin Sloan

Halloween is undoubtedly my favorite holiday of the year. As someone who's watched all the major horror movies, horror TV shows, and true crime documentaries, I love anything to do with the paranormal and spooky. So, when I discovered the show *Ghost Hunters*, I dove right in.

For the uninitiated, *Ghost Hunters* is a reality TV show where folks obsessed with the paranormal investigate allegedly haunted places to find ghosts. How do you uncover something invisible? Not by trying to locate it—at least not directly.

That's why ghost hunters use various equipment, like EMF meters and thermographic cameras, to detect signs of otherworldly activity. And while the jury is still out on the existence of ghosts, I find the ghost hunter approach fascinating.

Let's take a page out of their playbook by focusing our attention on the visible influence that the invisible exerts.

Here are a few markers of paranormal activity in the world of mental models:

- Have you ever wondered why some biases are unconscious?
- Why is it so difficult to learn new habits and unlearn old ones?
- Do you associate success with wealth? Why?
- Why is gifting diamonds considered the ultimate way to show you love someone, instead of something handmade that takes effort?
- Unless the relationship ended badly, why does it seem so unusual for people to be friends with their exes?

The answers to these questions reveal a common thread: ingrained ways of thinking. Whether they manifest in the stereotypes we unconsciously apply, ways of thinking we default to, or behaviors underpinned by nothing more than social norms and expectations, mental models influence our lives in countless ways.

Given how broadly applicable mental models are, there are dozens of ways to define them, including Peter Senge's view, which he shared in his book *The Fifth Discipline*, that "mental models are deeply ingrained assumptions, generalizations, or even pictures of images that influence how we understand the world and how we take action."

But perhaps a more practical definition for mental models is *patterns of thinking and understanding.* In other words, they closely resemble mindsets, worldviews, and ways of thinking of which we sometimes aren't consciously aware.

For example, if you were asked to describe a house to someone who doesn't know what that is, what would you say?

If you live in a developed nation, you might explain that a house is a structure people live in with a roof, doors, backyard, and windows. That's probably how I would convey what it is.

Now imagine someone who grew up in very different circumstances, perhaps in a shanty town within a developing nation. They may reply that a house is merely a space where family members reside, taking shelter from everything outside.

These two different ways of understanding the concept "house" are, in fact, mental models; they're the result of two unique, yet ingrained ways of thinking. What's beautiful is mental models are often specific to an individual.

That's because our mental models, or in this case our ingrained understanding of what a house means, are informed by our unique experiences, beliefs, exposures, and upbringings.

Unfortunately, these ingrained ways of thinking aren't always so harmless. They also act like filters, coloring the way we reason, understand the world, and behave whether we like it or not.

Mental models can be evolutionarily advantageous by helping us make quicker decisions—like how I turned that street corner to avoid a perceived threat. But they also bring into question whether those choices align with our actual values and goals instead of assumptions that've morphed into truths.

These ingrained ways of thinking can blind us to ideas challenging our deeply held beliefs, are not always accurate when generalized, and can limit us to familiar ways of thinking.

At this point, you may have some doubts. After all, these are big claims to make about a concept you've likely never heard of, but shapes how we think and make decisions, and plays a role in nearly every facet of our daily lives.

Once we're cognizant of these processes, however, we can begin to unpack whether they align with our beliefs and values, and if not, shift them accordingly. This can be a helpful tool in the modern world, considering how easily we are all connected.

HATING SOCIAL MEDIA

"Much of social media can be seen as the 'News of me.' It's not so much a platform for connecting and sharing as it is a platform for advertising the idea of yourself you want to portray to others: the image of yourself you want to project."

—*Hozier*

I used to hate social media. Hate is a strong word, and I don't throw it around lightly, but in my mind, social media deserved it.

I'm not sure when I first started feeling this way. I remember being excited to make my Facebook (which I'll use interchangeably with Meta) profile back in high school. I used to enjoy how much easier it made keeping in touch with people from my past who were no longer physically near me.

But the allure started wearing off after I began feeling that social media was nothing more than a highlight reel: a curated, unauthentic projection of our real, mundane lives. Keeping up a fake image, let alone a real one, never mattered to me to begin with. It all seemed like a monumental waste of time. I gradually stopped posting status updates, checking notifications, or scrolling on my feed.

Eventually, all that remained was wishing people happy birthday, participating in group chats, and accepting event invitations. It's safe to say at this point that my mental model of social media, or the way I unconsciously perceived it, was best characterized as *indifference*.

Over time, that indifference subtly transformed into distrust. The first straw was hearing how Russian troll farms and state-sponsored disinformation campaigns meddled in the 2016 election (Abrams 2019). Even after definitive proof surfaced, social media companies were reticent about their platforms' role, and it seemed like no one wanted to take responsibility for what happened.

Naturally, disinformation continued to spread unabated as social media platforms refused to take action and hid behind the challenges following any kind of content moderation. A few years later, the Cambridge Analytica scandal revealed how social media platforms and companies working with them abused our personal information (Confessore 2018).

Christopher Wylie, who worked with a Cambridge University academic to obtain the data, told the *Observer*: "We exploited Facebook to harvest millions of people's profiles. And built models to exploit what we knew about them and target their inner demons. That was the basis the entire company was built on" (Cadwalladr 2018).

While Facebook publicly denied it, their team was in fact aware personal information had been harvested on an unprecedented scale. They chose not to inform the 50 million people affected and did little to help them.

It shouldn't have been a surprise that this was allowed to happen considering how social media companies make money: *advertisements*. Ads based off your and my personal data—our likes, dislikes, interests, friends, and travel plans–which we never realized were being mined.

Now, my ingrained perception of social media transformed into *loathing*. My conversations with friends about social media inevitably led to vocalizing concerns over its negative impact on mental health and lack of guardrails.

After a few weeks of feeling this way, I decided to take a break from several platforms. I vowed to never use Instagram, no matter how disconnected I felt or how funny the memes were.

As if all of that wasn't bad enough, I later discovered social media is *designed* to be addicting. Just like gambling.

SOCIAL ADDICTION & THE MENTAL MODEL CYCLE

"Recognizing the cycle is the first step in freeing yourself from it."
—*Author Unknown*

Reading Nir Eyal's fantastic book *Hooked* opened my eyes to the ways social media platforms trigger dopamine rushes to hypnotize us, in what they call "maximizing engagement." *Hooked* presents a cycle of how social media works, tying each of the main activities to a step in the cycle.

Take a notification, for example, which can be understood as a kind of trigger or call to action. Because we don't know what the notification holds, our dopamine levels spike after we learn what the notification refers to and we're primed for more. The action we eventually take—like commenting on a post we're tagged in—yields a variable reward releasing even more dopamine. This ultimately culminates in an investment making the product more valuable to the user, and the cycle endlessly repeats itself.

Learning that statisticians who designed gambling machines architected social media platforms to follow this cycle was the last straw. The confluence of these experiences and exposures shaped my mental model of social media, or my ingrained way of thinking about it, into loathing—thinking social media is rife with problems and has resulted in more harm than good.

And upon further reflection, I realized mental models follow their own cycle as well.

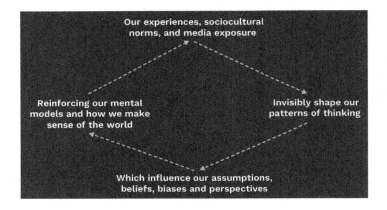

The Mental Model Cycle by Rohit Gupta

Over time the information I was exposed to—Russia's interference, the Cambridge Analytica scandal, and *Hooked*—coupled with my experiences working in cybersecurity for five years, shaped my view of social media from indifference to hatred.

But that process didn't happen all at once.

At first the changes were subtle—indifference turned into distrust—as my perception of social media shifted. Once that shifted, so did my unconscious beliefs, assumptions, and perspectives, ultimately manifesting in my reluctance to adopt Instagram.

This decision solidified my way of thinking, thanks to my heightened weariness of social media and predisposition to focus on its negative aspects.

Armed with this mental model, I was primed to focus on information that aligned with my mindset. For instance, I gravitated toward news like how Meta failed to stem racist abuse of England's soccer players, but subconsciously avoided a Harvard study which demonstrated a positive link between routine social media use and social well-being (Mac 2021; Roeder 2020).

The mental model continued reinforcing itself with passing time, making it extraordinarily difficult for me to notice how social media is used for good. And the cycle kept repeating.

Was there any way to avoid this vicious cycle? Undoubtedly. My initial pattern of thinking and the way it evolved would've been very different if I had more exposure to social media's benefits.

I know that for a fact because I've been using various social platforms more than ever these past few months to engage with folks who resonate with my ideas. It took me some time to unlearn and overcome my existing, reinforced way of thinking, but I'm glad I did.

A few months ago, I downloaded Instagram and started posting various forms of content regularly. I'm starting to understand how social media can be more than an echo chamber and actually expand our bubbles, and how making engaging content is an art form to be admired.

While understanding how my perception of social media shifted over time took years to understand, there's a mental model nearly everyone alive in the year 2020 developed: COVID-19's threat level.

RESPONDING TO COVID-19 NEWS

"The first thing is we have to get on the same page. We have to be united in one cause."

—*James P. Hoffa*

The COVID-19 pandemic is unlike those that came before it—like the Bubonic Plague and the Spanish Flu—for many reasons. But perhaps the most fascinating is that people can't agree on what to do in response to it. It's the first time in history that large groups of people have different ways of thinking about an outbreak, preventing us from getting on the same page with interventions like vaccinations or mask usage.

To unravel how that happened, let's examine reactions to COVID-19 and related updates through the lens of the mental model cycle. If you can, rewind to February 2020 or a couple weeks before the country you lived in went on lockdown.

When you first heard reports about this new virus spreading in Wuhan, what did you think? Were you worried about it?

At this point no one had formed thought patterns of COVID-19 because we didn't really know much about it. Instead, we unconsciously applied our pre-existing understanding of disease propagation and severity which, unless you work in epidemiology, probably instilled a sense of "how bad can it be?" After all, nothing in human history to date—not even swine flu or Ebola—could both spread quickly and kill efficiently (Rogers 2020).

It also didn't help that COVID-19 reports were scarce, unsurprising given how the Chinese Communist Party censors its own citizens, and American leadership downplayed the threat (Bump 2020). For all intents and purposes, it seemed like a tragic situation that the Chinese people and government had to deal with.

But as more information developed, stories reported, and exposure occurred, COVID mental models gradually diverged owing to our diverse backgrounds, surrounding sociocultural norms, and unique media exposure.

Without a doubt, there's a spectrum of mental models reflecting the various ways people have responded to COVID-19. But to generalize for a moment, let's assume there are largely two camps of people and each of them has wildly different ways of thinking.

Group A's mental model of COVID-19, shaped by their direct experiences, news exposure, the mental models of others in their community, and their existing ways of thinking, is that COVID-19 is like the flu. Their unconscious understanding is, "It's not really a problem for us and people seem to be making a really big deal out of nothing. I also don't trust the government's information about the virus."

A great example of someone belonging to Group A is Susan Wiles, a retired sign-language interpreter with an autoimmune disorder. Despite COVID-19 posing a significant risk to her health, she chose not to wear a mask when she walked into a Publix supermarket in Florida.

Susan was riding in a motorized cart in the produce department when a worker "jumped back," and gave her "a glaring look" (McKelvey 2020).

As she recalls, "He yelled: 'You're not wearing a mask.' It was quite a commotion. Another guy joined right in and said: 'She's a menace to society. Get her out of here.' Then he yells: 'Why don't you just go attend a Trump rally?'" (McKelvey 2020).

It turns out Susan has been to Trump's rallies. An avid Trump supporter, she chooses to not wear a mask, believing that concerns about COVID-19 are overblown. "Sure, there's a virus, [but] people die of the flu every year" (McKelvey 2020). When it comes to the pandemic, Susan confidently asserts, "I don't fall for this. It's not what they say it is" (McKelvey 2020).

And Susan isn't alone. David Aronoff, director of the Division of Infectious Diseases at Vanderbilt University Medical Center in Nashville, noted "there are other people who see masks as a violation of their rights. Some people don't wear masks because they say that they don't 'work'" (McKelvey 2020).

On the other hand, Group B's mental model of COVID-19, shaped by the same factors but very different contexts, is it *is* a big deal. Their unconscious understanding is, "this seems deadly, I have to be careful and make some real changes. I trust what the government is saying."

And just like how my initial mental model of social media was reinforced, each group's mental models gradually evolved as their unconscious assumptions, beliefs, and perspectives of COVID-19 changed.

In response to new stimuli—news reports, guidelines, etc.— these very different ways of thinking produced very different, tangible results. Take the hypothetical responses to the CDC's actual guidance below as an example:

CDC recommendation: Wearing masks limits the spread of the COVID-19 virus.

Group A: I don't trust the CDC. They've gone back and forth on this issue, and this doesn't make sense to me. From the cases I'm hearing and reading about, people who don't wear masks and continue their daily routines aren't getting infected. My friends and others in my community are just as skeptical as I am. I also can't stand being coerced by the government. I refuse to wear a mask.

Group B: I trust the CDC. Even though they've been back and forth previously, this is a definitive stance worth heeding. I'm not sure I fully understand how or why this works and I certainly don't like wearing masks, but if it makes me and others safer, I'll do it. I continue to see more cases on the news reinforcing the importance of masks. My friends and others in my community are doing it, too. I'll wear a mask.

When presented with new information—in this case updated CDC guidelines—each group applies its mental model to make sense of what's happening. The differing levels of mask adherence between the two groups reflects the distinct mental models each group formed. This played out in real life along political lines.

The Baltimore Sun reported in November 2020 that Democrats are more likely to wear masks than Republicans (76 percent versus 53 percent), even after controlling for differences in COVID-19 impacts in their communities. Individuals who reported voting for President Donald Trump in 2016 were "at least 25 percent less likely to wear a mask than individuals who did not" (Ryan 2020).

Once mental models are created, they act like a filter influencing how we think and feel, which in turn reinforces our mental models as we apply them to new experiences and exposures.

So, it should be no surprise that, as new developments in the war on COVID-19 occurred, people's behavior and their mental models themselves continued to diverge. Let's examine hypothetical responses to the below real news, released a few months after the CDC's recommendation.

New evidence from Pfizer: Vaccines are found to be more than 90 percent effective in preventing COVID-19.

Group A: Those vaccines were developed way too quickly. Something weird is going on here. COVID-19 isn't even that big of a deal, and my continued health proves it. I've also heard cases of some vaccines causing severe reactions, and I'm worried it'll happen to me. People in my community are continuing to go about their lives unvaccinated as well. I don't plan on getting vaccinated anytime soon.

Group B: It's incredible these vaccines were made so quickly. And 90 percent efficacy is amazing! I don't like getting them, but I generally get vaccinated. I'm seeing so many people I respect and trust get vaccinated, and it helps me trust that it's safe. I plan to get vaccinated as soon as I possibly can.

At this point, regardless of what group, mental models of COVID-19 have been reinforced and are incredibly difficult to shift. That's why, even though getting vaccinated may seem safe and straightforward to some, large groups of people responded very differently to vaccination news.

I sat down with Charles (name changed to respect his privacy), a friend and the doorman of my condo building, to discuss his view of vaccination. Charles is a Black man in his mid-fifties who lives in Oakland and grew up in Chicago. Our discussion is below, edited for length and clarity.

Rohit: Yeah, man, the last few days have been rough. Having COVID-19 sucks (I tested positive after a Tahoe trip), but I'm so glad I got vaccinated and received the booster shot. Have you been vaccinated?

Charles: So, I got the first two vaccinations, but I don't plan on getting a booster.

Rohit: Two of my friends I was with who also got COVID-19, but didn't get the booster, are having way worse symptoms: vomiting, 100-degree fevers, etc. It really seems to help with reducing symptom severity; would you reconsider?

Charles: No dude, I honestly don't need that shit. I keep myself healthy and don't go to parties or big gatherings—I live on my own and keep a tight circle. Plus, we don't even know the long-term effects of the vaccine yet!

Rohit: I get that, and I'm glad you're being safe, but why take the risk of COVID-19—which we know has painful short-term and sometimes long-term effects—versus a vaccine that millions have received without complication?

Charles: Honestly man, why should I trust the government? The government doesn't give a shit about any of us, and certainly not Black people. Do you know all the horrific things that've happened to Black people in the name of "science?" And just the other day a friend of mine was telling me this Assyrian guy he knows moved here a few months ago, and already has a convenience store he set up. Can you believe that? That'd never happen for a Black man. I was born here, lived here my whole life, have a stable job, and [have] upstanding character, [but] they would never give me a loan for a business like that.

Rohit: I'm sorry to hear that, man. I'm aware of some of the things that've happened and it's awful. Truly. But what

I don't understand is, the vaccine has been given to everyone: rich, poor, Black, and White. And if we agree that the government cares about White people, why would the government do something harmful to them?

Charles: The government doesn't care about anyone, dude. You think they would care about a few casualties of war? It's like the idea of being a victim of circumstance; no one will bat an eye about these things as long as it's in the name of the greater good.

Rohit: Even knowing that 99 percent of people who die from COVID-19 are unvaccinated? It seems safer to be unvaccinated than it actually is when we only hear from the people who survive, no? It's basically survivorship bias at play.

Charles: I don't buy it, man. I live a healthy lifestyle and nothing bad has ever happened. And I mean I *had* the thing back in October of 2020! That shit was nasty bro, like for real, I was mad coughing and felt like shit, but I still went to work. I still had to pay bills.

Rohit: Wait, so you even *had* COVID-19, felt the symptoms, and still decided to not get the booster shot despite that?

Charles: Yes, and I don't plan on changing that anytime soon.

When Charles first mentioned he didn't plan on getting a booster shot, I was shocked. We've had countless philosophical conversations about complex topics like the human condition, and although we don't always see eye to eye, I respect his way of thinking.

How could an intelligent, thoughtful person choose to put themselves in harm's way? Our conversation helped me realize how perception leads to action. The ingrained patterns of thinking we unknowingly develop strongly influence our thoughts and behavior, and if we apply the mental model cycle to Charles' mindset, it becomes clear why he feels the way he does.

His continued health, despite not receiving the booster shot, combined with exposure to the government's historic mistreatment of Black people, leads him to distrust the government. This way of thinking influences his perspective so when he's presented with a new circumstance—like the government endorsing multiple vaccines—he isn't convinced. And the mental model cycle keeps repeating.

Taking a step back, mental models are a great way to explain one's choices and thinking, and it's tempting to invoke them in any situation where thinking is involved. To avoid seeing nails everywhere, let's be more specific about the hammer we're using before we proceed.

THE TEN COMMANDMENTS OF MENTAL MODELS

"Say what you will about the ten commandments, you must always come back to the pleasant fact that there are only ten of them."
—*H.L. Mencken*

1. **They're learned**: These patterns of thinking are learned through imitation, informal schooling, and social conditioning. For instance, I wasn't born thinking success is defined by wealth, but I quickly learned through my parents' opinions, movies, and rap music.

2. **They're incomplete by design**: You can think of mental models as sketches of sorts. A simple sketch doesn't retain all the details of what it represents; consider what's left out in a stick figure sketch of a person. Despite not knowing much about how cars work, my pattern of thinking enables me to navigate the complex physics and interactions at play (like propulsion mechanics) to get from point A to point B.

3. **They're fluid**: Mental models are not static. They change when we learn new things, receive feedback challenging our existing mental models, or are exposed to people who think differently. But don't conflate fluidity with being easy to change. Recall that Amazon quickly responded to the introduction of e-books by promoting the Kindle e-reader. Borders, a big box bookstore, was slow to adapt and outsourced e-book sales to Amazon. Never heard of Borders before? That's because they went bankrupt in 2011 after failing to adjust their ways of thinking.

4. **They're based on beliefs**: Mental models are not based on facts but are rooted in one's experiences and assumptions,

shaped by the surrounding social, political, cultural, and ideological modes of thought. The underlying assumption is often wrong. For instance, if you saw a friend put their hand over a stove that's turned on, what do you predict will happen? Most people's ingrained way of thinking suggests their hand will burn—but what if it's an induction cooktop?

5. **They can work undercover**: Some mental models are invoked without one ever being cognizant of their existence. A different way to conceptualize them would be as ingrained patterns of thinking or worldviews. However, there's a plethora of mental models we can leverage on a day-to-day basis. Refer to Farnam Street's website to view 100 mental models you can consciously activate to make better decisions.

6. **They belong to individuals, groups, and organizations**: Every one of us has hundreds of mental models, but we also share thought patterns with people around us and those with whom we spend significant time. Shared mental models refer to a shared understanding between a group of people that shapes their behavior and understanding of their roles and beliefs. We'll explore this further in a later chapter. As we examined with Borders previously, organizations can possess shared ways of thinking as well.

7. **They're influencers**: Our ingrained ways of thinking encapsulate fundamental understandings or worldviews shaping the way we reason, perceive, and interact with our world.

8. **They simplify complexity**: Mental models are of particular importance for enabling understanding and navigation of our world. In many ways, they act like heuristics:

mental shortcuts facilitating problem-solving and probability judgments. These strategies are generalizations, or rules-of-thumb, that reduce cognitive load and are effective for making immediate judgments. Mental models abstract the complexity of our daily lives so we can focus on what matters.

9. **They're indestructible**: No matter how much we try, we will never get rid of mental models. That's not such a bad thing considering the benefits they provide, and it just means we should focus on reframing instead of eliminating them.

10. **They neglect what is false**: Our mental models only outline truths and neglect what they consider false. It's crucial that we take the necessary steps to ensure we haven't discarded thoughts, ideas, or information simply for contradicting our existing mental models. When traveling abroad, I've met folks my age who eschew traditional nine-to-five jobs and the lifestyles that come with them, and each time I felt strange because they're challenging the ingrained beliefs I have, rooted in capitalism and my upbringing, that one should stay at a high paying job for years before taking risks or enjoying life. It's imperative to consider why we've rejected perceived falsehoods contradicting our ingrained ways of thinking.

Keep these characteristics in mind when you try to identify mental models in your own life. Understanding how mental models are created, shaped, and reinforced is crucial in appreciating how difficult it is to change them, how they influence us invisibly, and how folks can behave very differently even when presented with the same information.

And maybe you're thinking of the million-dollar question: if we understand someone's mental models, or our own, can we change them? We'll get there.

THEY LIVE

"Put the glasses on! Put them on!"

—*John Nada*

One of my favorite movies of all time is the 1988 horror and sci-fi epic *They Live*, directed by the legendary John Carpenter.

The movie centers on the main character, a homeless drifter known as Nada (literally "nothing" in Spanish), coming to Los Angeles in search of work. Without spoiling too much of the movie—you should definitely watch it sometime—Nada eventually discovers a pair of sunglasses that don't seem to work; they make the world appear black and white.

Strange, right?

Turns out the glasses do something quite extraordinary: they reveal subliminal messages in the media guiding people to consume, reproduce, and conform.

My favorite scene happens shortly after Nada finds the sunglasses and begins putting them on while walking on a busy sidewalk. Without the glasses, he notices a big publicity billboard advocating for people to experience the holiday of a lifetime saying, "Come to the Caribbean," featuring a beautiful woman in a red bikini positioned underneath.

When Nada puts the sunglasses on, the billboard's message and picture are replaced with gray script on a pure white background with only the words, "Marry and Reproduce."

After that jarring experience, Nada begins to see subliminal messages everywhere hiding in plain sight. Like Nada, we all live our daily lives oblivious to the influence mental models have on us. My goal is to provide you sunglasses to see, with eyes unclouded by invisible filters, these thought patterns in action and recommend ways to alter the impact they have.

Now that we understand what mental models are, let's examine some of their benefits and drawbacks to better appreciate the role they play in our lives.

Thought Pattern Thoughts—Rohit Gupta

Keep uncovering thought patterns as you play
this endless game of finding your way

Discover ways to reframe
that the purpose of life isn't fame

Seeing beauty in the mundane
requires looking out a new windowpane

Confront ingrained beliefs and assumptions
all too often they result in corruption

Following footsteps can bring dismay
forge your own path no matter what others say

While challenging to see from a fresh perspective
it sparks much joy to cast a new narrative

And if you remember nothing else today
identify thought patterns getting in your way

REFLECTIONS

- Has your mental model of COVID-19's threat level changed over time? What factors do you think contributed to your initial perception, and what factors helped change it?
- How has your perception of social media changed over time? Why?
- Do you believe tattoos are unprofessional? If so, where does that belief stem from?
- What ways of thinking, shared by your parents or loved ones, have you realized you don't agree with?
- Have you ever thought that someone overweight must be unhealthy? What does weight have to do with health?

EXERCISES

- Share five mental models influencing your thinking or behavior of which you aren't typically cognizant. These can be related to your career, lifestyle choices, biases and predispositions, perceptions, and more.

_____
_____
_____
_____
_____

- For each of the mental models you wrote down, jot down a list of situations and circumstances where they may manifest to help identify them. Using an association of success with wealth and happiness as an example, situations I'd look out for include: thinking about my next career step, existential crises over what I'm actually passionate about, discussions with my parents about my life plans and their viewpoint, conversations with friends about the joy having or spending money brings, and more.

_____

_____

_____

_____

_____

Benefits & Drawbacks

"Life isn't black and white. It's a million gray areas, don't you find?"

—RIDLEY SCOTT

What's something that helps and hurts us, but we just can't seem to get enough?

There's no right or wrong answer here. Everything from spicy food, knowledge, and even popping pimples fit the bill. But what immediately pops up in my mind is: drugs. No matter if it's weed, alcohol, coffee, or something else—using substances to change our mental states has obvious benefits and drawbacks.

In a way, our use of mental models is like using drugs. Take drinking for example. Imbibing in a few glasses of wine— or your alcohol of choice—can reduce stress, increase happiness, and make social situations far more pleasant (Baum-Baicker 1985). But doing so can also increase weight, lead to depression, and cause bad hangovers (Baum-Baicker 1985).

Mental models are no different. On one hand, these patterns of thinking are critical survival tools, aid problem solving, and improve teamwork and coordination; on the other hand, they can lead us to see patterns where there are none or misapply them, stymie innovation, and reinforce social boundaries.

To truly understand the role that mental models play in our lives, we must first learn to appreciate their broader benefits and drawbacks.

Note: While much of this book is focused on patterns of thinking we unconsciously rely on, this chapter includes benefits of mental models that we consciously apply.

THE KEY TO SURVIVING, THRIVING, AND USING MUGS

"The difference in mind between man and the higher animals, great as it is, is certainly one of degree and not of kind."
—*Charles Darwin*

Why did *Homo sapiens*, out of dozens of humanlike species, survive and become the dominant life form on planet Earth? It wasn't because of our opposable thumbs.

Many species boast these dexterous digits, like koalas, gorillas, and even pandas, and some studies suggest hominids of the genus *Australopithecus* possessed this adaptive appendage millions of years ago (Tishmack 2018; Handwerk 2021).

Certainly, our supremacy isn't the result of our physical strength or sense of smell, but I'd argue the factor which played the biggest role in our evolution and ability to adapt to new circumstances was pattern recognition.

Why?

Say ten wolves are lurking around the corner. Four hunters can hardly fight them. In this case, the hunters should opt to stay back and wait.

The hunters only know this, though, if they can correctly estimate how many wolves await them; if they mistake the sounds of ten wolves for one, they face certain death. Their ability to differentiate the pattern of sounds and environmental cues between ten wolves and one enables them to make crucial decisions that aid survival.

The same can be said for foraging berries.

Recalling and distinguishing which kinds of berries, based on shape, color, texture, and smell, are not poisonous greatly improves odds of survival.

In these ways, pattern recognition—or the art and science of using our memory, knowledge, and past experience to understand the world around us—is one of the biggest evolutionary advantages for human beings.

Whether it's encountering a stranger in a dark alley or perceiving a wild animal nearby, activating learned patterns of thinking can be the difference between life and death. Observing and applying patterns wasn't just crucial to survival in prehistoric times, it paved a way forward in the past few decades as well.

So much of modern technology relies on biomimicry. Everything from airplanes (designed around how birds fly) to solar power (designed around how plants convert sunlight into energy) are based on patterns we've observed in nature and replicated through science.

In some cases, we've gone a step further and developed our own patterns as well—like the computer software enabling me to write this very book or neural networks which even surpass chess grandmasters in skill (Silver et al. 2018).

Beyond patterns we're cognizant of, our ingrained patterns of thinking help us on a day-to-day basis. Even something as mundane as using mugs. There are millions of different mugs: different sizes, colors, shapes, materials, uses, etc. But we understand a mug is a mug because we recognize the characteristics that make it such. That's why we recognize and understand how to use a mug at any point, even if it looks different every time.

Imagine for a second a world where, every time we look at a different mug, we must learn how to use it all over again.

We'd move much more slowly in the world, and our problem-solving abilities would be way more limited. How can we recognize different versions of mugs without ever having seen them before?

Our ability to identify never-before-seen mugs isn't magic, but rather the result of a pattern we've internalized by building a cognitive representation, or mental model, of what a mug is and how to use it. Through our experiences and conditioning, we learn to recognize new objects as mugs by identifying shapes suggesting they can hold something and sizes reflecting they can be held in one hand. The same capability enables us to use complex tools, regardless of variations in shape, size or color, to meet our daily needs, whether that tool be a vehicle, mug, or weapon.

While we should all be thankful mental models exist to help us navigate complexities and difficult situations, we must also be wary of how they can lead us to apply patterns where there are none or misapply them altogether.

SAMURAI IN CRABS AND PEOPLE ON MARS

"Psychologists have long known that people see patterns where none exist."

—*Michael Lewis*

The year was 1185, the place a tiny bay called Dan-no-ura. Two great fleets faced one another: on one side, the Heike clan, imperial rulers of Japan, and on the other, the Minamoto, upstarts fighting to control the throne.

At stake was control of all Japan.

After a half-day of fighting, the Heike were routed, and their six-year-old emperor was drowned by his subjects to keep him out of Minamoto hands.

A strange story arose in the wake of the battle. Locals told a legend about crabs in the area, Heikegani, with strange patterns on their shells said to resemble samurai masks. Legend held that the crabs were the reincarnations of samurai slain at the Battle of Dan-no-ura (Kincaid 2013).

If you're able to look up Heikegani and see what they look like, take a close look at the crab's shell—do you see a samurai face? Even if you don't, why do our brains work this way?

Unfortunately, or maybe fortunately, there are no ghost crabs. Turns out there are tons of other crab species with similar patterns, although maybe not as pronounced. The samurai face is the byproduct of folds and creases where the crab's muscles attach to its shell. People just happen to think they look like faces or masks.

Seeing samurai faces in the shells of Heikegani beautifully illustrates a phenomenon called *pareidolia:* our tendency to find significance in random or vague things. It's just like when people thought they saw a face on Mars back in 2001; some reported an "enormous head nearly two miles from end to end seemed to be staring back at the cameras from a region of the Red Planet called Cydonia" (Philips 2001).

In both cases our perception turned out to be distorted, but these examples beg a simple question: are there downsides to recognizing patterns too well? Or seeing patterns where none actually exist?

It depends on the pattern and how or when we apply it. Problems arise when a pattern is born out of distorted exposure, applied indiscriminately, and influenced by ideology.

Take algorithmic bias as an example. Twitter recently announced the results of an algorithmic bug bounty competition—a virtual race to find issues in the company's algorithms—revealing that Twitter's cropping algorithm favors faces that are "slim, young, of light or warm skin color and smooth skin texture, and with stereotypically feminine facial traits" (Vincent 2021).

The second- and third-placed entries "showed that the system was biased against people with white or gray hair, suggesting age discrimination, and favors English over Arabic script in images" (Vincent 2021).

Rumman Chowdhury, director of Twitter's META team (which studies Machine learning Ethics, Transparency, and Accountability), uses the phrase "life imitating art imitating life."

She argues that "we create these filters because we think that's what beauty is, and that ends up training our models and driving these unrealistic notions of what it means to be attractive" (Vincent 2021). I think she hits the nail on the head, but I'd amend what she said just slightly: our *invisible filters* (mental models) shape our conception of beauty, resulting in ways of thinking reinforcing our ingrained beliefs which themselves are based on sociocultural norms and ideological pressures.

Misapplying patterns is also responsible for why home loan approvals are so difficult to obtain for people of color. An investigation by The Markup revealed lenders—increasingly relying on app-based loan origination solutions—were more likely to deny home loans to people of color than to White people with similar financial characteristics (Hale 2021).

Specifically, "80 percent of Black applicants are more likely to be rejected, along with 40 percent of Latino applicants, and 70 percent of Native American applicants are likely to be denied" (Hale 2021).

Replicating patterns not based on truth and applying them indiscriminately are unfortunate byproducts of our mental models. We must actively fight our urges to find significance in random events, because while seeing samurai in crabs or faces on Mars may seem harmless, our tendencies to view people as threats and stereotype the world around us are not.

SECRET OF THE SUCCESSFUL: SOLVING HARD PROBLEMS

"We cannot solve our problems with the same thinking we used when we created them."

—*Albert Einstein*

At the tender age of sixteen, a precocious Albert Einstein started contemplating what would happen if he were to chase after a beam of light.

If you could keep pace with it, the light must appear stationary, he imagined. Its shifting electric and magnetic fields would be frozen. But that seemed impossible. The equations developed by James Maxwell forbid it, and there's never been such a thing as frozen light.

"One sees in this paradox the germ of the special relativity theory is already contained," he wrote in 1947 (Battersby 2016). As Einstein came to realize from this experiment, the motion of light is the same no matter how fast you are moving. Even if you were traveling at almost the speed of light, the ray would still zip away from you at the same constant speed.

This idea, a rejection of his former way of thinking about the nature of light in consideration of a new one, eventually led Einstein to an entirely new way of seeing the universe through the equations of special relativity. Although the thought experiment on its own didn't lead to Einstein's groundbreaking discovery, it helped him realize the untenability of the previously accepted emission theory of light.

Einstein's many thought experiments helped him find anomalies and inconsistencies in prevailing theories, enabling a reorientation of the patterns of thinking he previously relied upon. By adjusting his mental model, Einstein arrived at a framework correctly explaining the physics phenomena he envisioned.

If Einstein were alone in this, his mental simulation habit could be chalked up to a mere personal quirk. But as one digs deeper, a pattern emerges in how many of history's greatest inventors and scientists utilized mental simulation to make discoveries.

From a young age, Nikola Tesla developed an aptitude for conjuring imaginary people, societies, and worlds. He described how he would spend hours each night traveling in his own mind, meeting people, seeing new cities and countries, and making friends.

By the time he was seventeen, he had practiced the art of mental simulation so much that he found it easy to turn this skill toward his own inventions:

> When I get an idea, I start at once building it up in my imagination. I change the construction, make improvements and operate the device in my mind. It is absolutely immaterial to me whether I run my turbine in thought or test it in my shop. I even note if it is out of balance. There is no difference whatever, the results are the same. In this way I am able to rapidly develop and perfect a conception without touching anything. When I have gone so far as to embody in the invention every possible improvement I

can think of and see no fault anywhere, I put into concrete form this final product of my brain. Invariably my device works as I conceived that it should, and the experiment comes out exactly as I planned it. In twenty years, there has not been a single exception (Tesla 1919).

I doubt my thought experiments will ever be as precise as Tesla's, but the beautiful thing about them as a tool is they don't need to be. By forcing you to vividly confront or visualize your patterns of thinking, they help unlock new perspectives crucial to solving difficult problems.

Challenging his patterns of thinking enabled Tesla to develop countless incredible inventions, including the alternating current motor, radio, hydroelectric power generation, and many more. Thought experiments are amazing tools we can all leverage to augment our problem-solving capabilities.

As Farnam Street Media points out on their blog:

Thought experiments are powerful because they help us learn from our mistakes and avoid future ones. They let us take on the impossible, evaluate the potential consequences of our actions, and re-examine history to make better decisions. They can help us both figure out what we really want, and the best way to get there.

Successful problem solving, especially involving new problems or situations, relies on challenging existing ways of thinking through thought experiments or by constructing accurate representations that properly frame the problem.

But sadly, solely relying on ingrained ways of thinking can stymie problem solving rather than improve it.

INNOVATION INERTIA

"Now typically what we do is we take our thinking patterns and extend it to find new solutions. So, if your thinking pattern is the airplane, you might want to extend it...But you can't extend an airplane into a space rocket, they're fundamentally different systems of propulsion...Extending your current method of thinking isn't sufficient to get breakthrough ideas."

—*Paul Sloane*

The enemy of most large companies is the ingrained mindset of doing things *the way it's always been*. From Blockbuster to Borders (RIP), history has proven companies with innovation inertia are destined to have their lunch eaten by faster, hungrier competitors.

We all know *what* happened in the cases of Blockbuster and Borders. But what's more interesting to dissect is *why* those companies failed to adapt with the times, even when the writing was clearly on the wall.

It wasn't because they were incapable of innovating. Rather, they *chose* not to—blinded by their ingrained ways of thinking preventing them from realizing their business models and distribution methods would quickly become obsolete.

Once Blockbuster CEO, John Antioco, became convinced that Netflix and Redbox were threats, he used his authority, as well as the credibility he had earned by nearly doubling Blockbuster's revenues during his tenure, to discontinue the late fees annoying customers and invested heavily into a digital platform to ensure the brand's future.

Although he convinced the board to back his plan, one of Antioco's lieutenants, Jim Keyes, mounted a last-ditch effort to do things the way they'd always been done. He pointed out that the costs of Antioco's changes, about $200 million to drop late fees and another $200 million to launch "Total Access" (an online version of Blockbuster which resembled Netflix), were damaging profitability (Satell 2021).

It didn't take long before an activist investor, Carl Icahn, began to question Antioco's leadership. Antioco ultimately lost the board's confidence and was fired over a compensation dispute in 2005. His lieutenant, Jim Keyes, was named CEO and immediately reversed his predecessor's changes. Blockbuster went bankrupt five years later.

The same activist investor Carl Icahn would later write:

> *Keyes felt the company couldn't afford to keep losing so much money, so we pulled the plug. To this day I don't know what would have happened if we'd avoided the big blowup over Antioco's bonus and he'd continued growing Total Access. Things might have turned out differently (Satell 2021).*

What's most surprising is that Blockbuster's eventual bankruptcy wasn't due to a lack of innovation or Netflix's strategic maneuvering. The company had the resources and ingenuity to shift to a digital future but didn't act on it. Blockbuster went under because its management couldn't shift its ingrained ways of thinking.

Perhaps an even more poignant example is Kodak, a technology company that dominated the photographic film market during most of the twentieth century.

The company blew its chance to lead the digital photography revolution all because their mental models blinded them to the possibility of a filmless future. Steve Sasson, a Kodak engineer, invented the first digital camera back in 1975.

"But it was filmless photography, so management's reaction was, 'that's cute—but don't tell anyone about it,'" said Sasson (Deutsch 2008). The leaders of Kodak failed to see digital photography as a disruptive technology because their deeply rooted patterns of thinking restrained them to only seeing possibilities with film.

A former vice-president of Kodak, Don Strickland, later said, "We developed the world's first consumer digital camera, but we could not get approval to launch or sell it because of fear of the effects on the film market" (Usborne 2012).

The management was so focused on film success, they missed the digital revolution—after starting it themselves. Kodak eventually filed for bankruptcy in 2012.

While applying the right model to a problem can be helpful, ingrained ways of thinking can cause innovation inertia by constraining thinking and understanding. And just like companies, people can quickly find themselves in hot water if they fail to shift their mental models.

The last internship I had in college before joining the real world was with a large, global Swiss bank known as Credit Suisse. I had the pleasure of working in the investment banking team, which meant working an average of one hundred hours per week in an extremely fast-paced and stressful environment.

A key feature of investment banking is the hardened hierarchy and chain of command. Interns report to analysts, who review their work and report to associates, who report to VPs, then principals, and, ultimately, partners. At each stage in the chain, the individual gains more autonomy; at the intern level, we were pretty much told what to do.

All we had to do was execute. So, you can imagine what a shock it was transitioning from that environment—with the mindset I developed—to an extremely flat, early-stage startup with just twenty people.

In my first job out of college, I joined a cybersecurity startup, ShieldX Networks, as the second hire on the product management team. I held a lot of responsibility with limited oversight. At times, it felt like I was a fish that somehow ended up on dry land.

The friction I felt while dealing with my newfound autonomy helped me realize the ways of thinking I had unknowingly hardened as an investment banker—spending as little brain power thinking about what to do and just focusing on execution—were not only useless, but actually harmful.

I recall a painful conversation with my now-deceased and once-in-a-lifetime manager, John Parker, a few weeks after I started. He shared:

"Rohit, you're clearly a bright guy. From the conversations we have about work and other things, that much is clear. So, I don't understand why you keep asking me for what you should work on or do next. It's not *my* job to tell you that. It's *yours*. You're clearly competent enough to figure out what to do, so try doing that!"

It didn't even occur to me that I wasn't performing well, and I was shocked to discover John was growing frustrated with my behavior. Because of the mental model I developed from my investment banking internship, I thought finishing tasks quickly and asking for more work would make me seem eager and capable.

But turns out, it just made me seem incompetent! Although it took a few months, I flipped my way of thinking and became comfortable creating my own agenda and developing new processes without guidance from John. That conversation underscored for me the importance of not relying on familiar mental models, and how doing so can cause problems rather than help solve them.

TEAMWORK TO MAKE THE DREAM WORK

"A successful team is a group of many hands but of one mind."
—*Bill Bethel*

There's nothing like a crisis for bringing multi-disciplinary groups of people together. Consider the case of the thirty-three Chilean miners who found themselves trapped 700 meters below ground after a collapse near their worksite in 2010.

A crack team of specialists from the mining company, the Chilean government, the Chilean Navy, geological organizations around the globe, and even NASA assembled virtually overnight. They worked around the clock for over two months until every miner was back above ground and reunited with their family (Pallardy 2010).

Fortunately, when most of us engage in cross-disciplinary work, the stakes aren't nearly as high. But according to Dr. Amy Edmondson, co-author of the book *Extreme Teaming*, many of the factors that led to the rescue operation's success also play a role in the success of everyday workplace teams.

She specifically noted:

1. The rescue team had a clear mission with adaptable success measures (bring the miners up alive, or failing that, deliver their bodies to the families).
2. They had the right expertise and the autonomy to do their jobs the best way they knew how.

3. And perhaps most importantly, they shared mental models of the timeline for their work (ASAP), their priorities (human lives over monetary or ecological cost), and how the contributions of each expert fit into the operation as a whole (Goff-Dupont 2020).

Shared mental models go a long way toward taking the friction out of cross-functional collaboration. Within the context of teamwork, shared mental models revolve around the roles and responsibilities of team members, the flow of information, and how they interact with each other based on each member's skills and preferences. The common understanding and mutual predictability that comes from having shared ways of thinking help teams collaborate smoothly.

One surprising result of shared mental models is a decrease in communication. While generally important to teamwork, studies found the counter-intuitive result that the higher-performing teams communicate less in high-tempo or high workload scenarios (Yen et al. 2003).

And this dynamic was attributed to greater implicit coordination made possible through shared mental models. Similarly, higher-performing teams tend to have cultures in which team members with more bandwidth proactively help others who are overloaded and often do so without explicit communication. Shared mental models play a crucial role by providing the basis for mutual awareness.

The core idea is that mental models help team members predict what their teammates are going to do and need. A shared mental model enables team members to form accurate explanations and expectations for the task and adapt their behavior in response to changing demands and other team members' needs.

An important point to note is the shared mental model theory does not imply that the team members have identical ways of thinking or understanding; rather, the crucial implication is that team members hold compatible mental models leading to common expectations for the task and team. And the positive benefits shared mental models bring to team situations have been investigated deeply. A study from the *Indian Journal of Critical Care Medicine* showed a remarkable increase in survival to hospital charge—from 23 percent to 69 percent—when teams completed ACLS (advanced cardiac life support) training (Project Hearbeat 2018). When teams learn together and are encouraged to develop a shared mental model through ACLS training, performance, team coordination, and adaptability under stress are greatly improved (Müller 2021).

It's clear that shared mental models are critical to the success of high performing groups, including cardiac critical care teams, military combat specialists, and even hunters working together in silence.

What may not be apparent, however, is how these shared ways of thinking reinforce undesirable social boundaries.

SHARED UNDERSTANDINGS: MAINTAINING SOCIAL BOUNDARIES

"You only are free when you realize you belong no place—you belong every place—no place at all. The price is high. The reward is great."

—Maya Angelou

Shared mental models can be powerful tools enabling groups of people or teams to feel a sense of unity and work together seamlessly. Unfortunately, they can also heighten social boundaries and divisions, as we'll see is the case with pilgrimages.

Pilgrimage broadly refers to the practice of journeying to sites where religious powers, knowledge, or experience are deemed especially accessible. In the Hindu tradition, pilgrimage is rooted in ancient scriptures including the epic *Mahabharata* and several of the Puranas (encyclopedic collections of myth, legend, and genealogy composed in Sanskrit). While the messages vary from text to text, they all elaborate on the capacities of sacred sites to grant boons, such as health, wealth, progeny, and deliverance after death. Some texts enjoin Hindu pilgrims to perform rites on behalf of ancestors and recently deceased kin. And Sanskrit sources as well as devotional literature in regional languages praise certain places and their miraculous capacities.

By some estimates, over 300 million individuals undertake pilgrimages to visit the world's key religious sites annually (UNWTO 2014). Hampi, a dainty temple village in the Indian state Karnataka, is a great example of a sacred pilgrimage site.

You wouldn't know it today, but Hampi was once the royal capital and religious center of the Vijayanagar Empire, one of the greatest empires in India's history. Hampi continues to draw a myriad of tourists owing to its temples, monolithic sculptures, and remarkable monuments; it doesn't hurt to be listed as a World Heritage Site by UNESCO either.

There are many amazing temples located in Hampi in various states of repair, and while most visitors come to take in the site collectively, there are two must-see standouts: the Virupaksha temple and the Vitthala temple. The Virupaksha temple is considered a "gem" of Vijayanagara architecture, and it served as the centerpiece of pilgrimages for thousands of Hindus and Jains. It's precisely these kinds of pilgrimages that Dr. Alexandra Mack, author of the book *Spiritual Journey, Imperial City: Pilgrimage to the Temples of Vijayanagara*, set out to understand further.

Dr. Mack argues that pilgrimage serves two seemingly opposed social functions—social separation and social integration—and these social factors can be seen through the examination of spatial and economic evidence. To test this hypothesis, she and her team evaluated maps using geographic information systems in addition to inscriptions that recorded monetary and physical gifts to temples. After analyzing the data further, Dr. Mack shared:

> *While it appears that pilgrimage to Vijayanagara engendered communitas among and between pilgrims, the archaeological record indicates that most other relationships in and around the temples were characterized by their inequality. In fact, pilgrimage appears to have*

highlighted and reinforced many social boundaries in society.... At Vijayangara, pilgrims were separated from residents both spatially and economically. The routes of movement through the Vithala temple district, while ritualized, were also focused on keeping outsiders away from private, residential areas. Visitors were also restricted in what resources, such as water, they could access.... The issue of social separation is also evident in the relationships between the pilgrims and elites who could donate to temples. In addition to the unequal gifting relationship, elites were separated from pilgrims and from many of the local residents simply because they were wealthy and had the means to have their wealth and generosity proclaimed in stone. As artifacts, inscriptions provide key insights into how elites separated themselves from each other, using donations to the temples as expressions of identity and claims to power (Mack 2010).

For much of my life, I've always believed pilgrimages erase social boundaries as individuals join together to undertake a shared, spiritual journey. But Dr. Mack's research illustrates how social boundaries are maintained in a variety of subtle ways, ranging from restricting access to certain areas to unequal relationships regarding charity.

It's fascinating how shared mental models, while seemingly erasing individual identity in lieu of a shared identity or experience, maintain our social divisions. Shared mental models reinforce perceptions of one's role in a larger group, just as pilgrimages to Hampi's temples did. And so, the same dynamic enabling emergency room staff or cardiac teams to work together effectively is also responsible for cliché nurse-doctor antagonisms. Despite relying on them to close the loop in patient care and coordinating with them effectively, doctors look down on nurses as being a support function in the shared healthcare mental model.

Ria Hanna, a retired nurse, recounts a harrowing time when she was made to feel like an inferior part of the patient care team by a physician:

A patient began bleeding during surgery and the surgeon called for a [blood draw]. This particular test has a very stringent protocol about how it is drawn, how it is labeled, etc. or the blood bank will refuse it, and it must be redrawn. This is also a stopgap measure to make sure the patient is not inadvertently put in danger. I stepped around the patient to draw her blood and the surgeon huffed and puffed [saying] that this was ridiculous, drew a tube of blood from her anesthesia line and practically threw it at me. 'Get it down there!' He screamed. [After] tactfully informing him that the blood bank would not accept this tube without proper procedure being followed… the doctor threw his instruments down and began screaming at me saying that I was a nurse, an errand girl, a nothing, and he…HE was a doctor, a veritable GOD of the hospital, and I needed to learn to do what I was TOLD (Hanna 2020).

Ria's story is heart-wrenching, but she's not the only one. Doctor-nurse hierarchies are well defined in many hospitals despite the sense of unity toward a common mission, effective coordination, and awareness at play. A survey conducted by the Institute for Safe Medication Practices in 2012 found that 87 percent of surveyed nurses encountered physicians who refused to answer their questions or return calls, 74 percent received condescending or demeaning comments from physicians, and 26 percent had objects thrown at them by doctors (Robbins 2015).

If all that wasn't bad enough, physicians shamed, humiliated, or spread malicious rumors about 42 percent of the surveyed nurses (Robbins 2015). A New York-based critical care nurse even told Alexandra Robbins, author of *The Nurses: A Year of Secrets, Drama, and Miracles with the Heroes of the Hospital*, that "every single nurse I know has been verbally berated by a doctor. Every single one" (Robbins 2015). That's not to say most doctors treat nurses poorly, but these behaviors seem far more common than initially expected.

Turning back to the Hindu homeland, India has another great example of how shared understandings maintain social boundaries: the caste system. We'll explore the mental models and dynamics at play there in a later chapter.

While it's incredible that shared mental models promote unity and teamwork, we should be concerned that they maintain and reinforce social boundaries. Perhaps the natural tradeoff between enabling working together as a cohesive whole, understanding intimately the role each part plays, is a hyperawareness of those roles and the value we ascribe to them.

Mental models clearly played an outsized role in our ability to survive, solve problems, and work together effectively.

But they also lead to bias, impede innovation, and maintain social boundaries. It's critical we perceive mental models as tools in a toolbox—they can be effective or cause problems depending on how we use them. In the next chapter, we'll examine the role mental models play in successfully changing behavior.

Mental Model Haiku—Rohit Gupta

Recognizing mugs
Everyday superpower
Taken for granted

Samurai in crabs
Like a Rorschach inkblot test
Man's search for meaning

Solving hard problems
Experiment with your thoughts
Challenge assumptions

Innovate or die
So never stop asking why
We think how we do

Shared understandings
Tacit but somehow so strong
Silence is the proof

Celebrate teammates
So no places must be known
We are all needed

REFLECTIONS

- What's one way pattern recognition helps you in your daily life, and what's one way it creates problems?
- Besides Blockbuster, Borders, and Kodak, what's another business that went out of business because it chose to do things the way they've always been done?
- What are three ways mental models help you navigate the complexity of your daily life?
- What's a mental model you share with others? This could be with your friends, family, coworkers, etc.
- Why do ingrained ways of thinking reinforce our "place"—whether that's in the context of our careers, families, or social settings?

EXERCISES

- Think of a problem you've encountered recently to which you couldn't find an answer. How could shifting your mental model help solve it?
- Everyone has some degree of pareidolia. How intense is yours? Take this quiz here: https://bzfd.it/3plH5Cg or search for "Buzzfeed pareidolia quiz" on Google to find out.
- To get a sense of how to use a thought experiment to test an idea, consider Hobbes' Ship of Theseus experiment: there is a very well-used boat. During the life of a ship, parts break down and are replaced. The mast, for instance, is lost in a storm and so they get a new one, some of the wood rots and is replaced with fresh timber, and the bolts and nails holding it together rust away and are replaced

with fresh bolts and nails. Eventually, none of the original materials that made up the ship are there. Yet, the boat still sails, same as ever. Is this the same boat or a different boat now?

- — Once you've reached your own conclusion, think of your own thought experiment to test one of your beliefs, assumptions, or hypotheses.

To Change or Not to Change?

"If you want to change, you have to be willing to be uncomfortable."

—AUTHOR UNKNOWN

Human beings are creatures of habit.

This age-old adage speaks to a fundamental truth of the human condition: our behavior is hard to change. Losing weight, confronting bias, and unlearning undesirable habits are just a few examples of behaviors many struggle to adjust. Why is it so hard to accomplish these goals, and what can we do about it?

Recall the embarrassing encounter I shared previously: turning right instinctively to avoid a group of Black men because I associated them with danger. Changing this behavior requires more than simply being aware of this bias. It necessitates acknowledging that any behavior is driven by ingrained patterns of thinking, and I need to take steps to adjust those patterns.

Now we've learned *what* a mental model is and *why* they can be useful or harmful, our next goal is to appreciate *how* they can be applied to understand the nuances of different situations.

And an examination of farmers' reluctance to adopt beneficial practices, Chrysler's recall of over a million vehicles, and Ecuador's failed "Todos somos mestizos" campaign reveal how an understanding of mental models is crucial to driving behavior change for groups of people.

Changes that sometimes make the difference between life and death.

SAVING SMALL FARMS

"Be determined, not stubborn."

—*Author Unknown*

Small farms are vanishing at an alarming pace in the United States (McGreal 2019). A shrinking farming population, government intervention which only supports commodity crops, an emergence of highly efficient grocery systems, and the rise of agribusinesses like Monsanto are the meteors to blame for the mass extinction.

Collectively, the nation lost over 100,000 farms between 2011 and 2018, with 12 percent of that happening in the last two years studied (Semuels 2019). At one point during the height of the COVID-19 pandemic, a third of small farms were close to going bankrupt and recovery has been slow (Meyer 2020).

Why does this matter? Isn't it a good thing that the Monsantos of the world are driving crop prices down?

It turns out that small farms are vital to our economy and well-being as a nation. They not only support the sustainability of rural economies, but also protect and enhance the environment, provide a nursery for the development of new enterprises, and help maintain rural populations.

That's why researchers at UC Davis and the University of Connecticut felt compelled to investigate the situation further.

Specifically, they set out to explore the nature of ingrained patterns of thinking related to farming among small farm operators in the northeastern United States where pressures on small family farms are especially intense.

By doing so, they hoped to understand the ways farmers perceive their world and aid educators working to help small farm operators overcome barriers to their success.

Over the course of six months from February to August of 2002, the researchers conducted interviews to understand "farmers' perceptions of the different types of knowledge they possessed, ways they developed their knowledge, and how they went about solving problems and making decisions" (Eckert 2005).

Before we explore some of their findings, let's pause to contemplate what mental models mean in the context of farming. They include the individual's values and beliefs about the ideal and the actual state of farming, the role and relative importance of one's beliefs and knowledge, and ways of processing information and applying skills to learn and solve problems.

For instance, Carla's mental model of farming, firmly rooted in the old ways, led her to initially reject advice from experts she felt was at odds with her mental model.

She recounts an experience she had asking for advice after noticing her tomatoes were dropping down prematurely:

> *When I called the [names university] guy about the tomatoes that were dropping down dead…I explained to him what they looked like, what happens, he started giving me a solution. Well, I'm not gonna spray that…I'm not gonna do that…Then he remembered who I was. [The university guy shared that] you wanna go get some Epsom salts and put it in a little sprayer and spray a little bit of Epsom salts on it…. It was a magnesium deficiency because the nights had gotten cold, and the tomatoes had used up all the available magnesium in the potting soil (Eckert 2005).*

In response to a further question about the expert's first suggestion to use a nonorganic chemical, Carla answered:

Right. Some chemical that had some other anti-fungal [properties] because they were more likely to get a fungus and some other things. But he told me how to cope with that: open a door, air out the greenhouse, don't let the humidity get high in the next couple of days, don't kick the heat up, drop it down a little more so that you're not having those big fluctuations. He gave me some things I could do that worked perfectly fine...So there were alternatives. He knew what they were (Eckert 2005).

The mental models that farmers like Carla form guide them in seeking information and deciding what feedback and advice to accept, reject, or adapt, and inform how to act and make decisions. In general, farmers—as do the rest of us—act in line with ingrained patterns of thinking based on values, beliefs, and knowledge they feel are important.

Unfortunately, this led to some farmers rejecting expert advice when it didn't fit with their mental model of farming. Instead, they would seek further evidence matching their mindset, a classic case of confirmation bias.

A perfect example of this behavior in action is Ellen, an organic farmer, who described her reaction to expert advice that didn't fit with her mental model rooted in the natural aspect of farming:

The year before when we had so much rain, I was very concerned about nitrogen leaching in the field [because] with so much rain it just leaches through and then the crops don't have enough nitrogen.... So we put compost down and that's it, we don't add fertilizer, we don't have any amendments that we use, so we don't have a quick fix for anything. So, if there's low nitrogen, even a lot of organic farms will go to Chilean nitrate or something like that which is a quick fix of nitrogen…I don't believe in that. So, I took some soil samples and sent them to…get it soil tested and we [received] a call. This guy was…telling me how low our nitrogen level is, and nothing's gonna grow [unless you put in Chilean nitrate]. And I thanked him very much and hung up…I don't care what the soil test has to say, I'm not gonna do that…I'm not gonna go and put stuff on my fields that don't fit the problem (Eckert 2005).

Both Ellen and Carla view farming through a natural lens and have a hard time adopting practices clashing with that thought pattern. Ellen's aversion to the expert's advice, just like Carla's hesitancy to spray her tomatoes with a non-organic chemical, illustrates the importance of aligning to others' mental models to affect change. Farmers are much more likely to listen to ideas aligning with their own.

While it may seem unique to farmers, we all behave in a similar way—rejecting thoughts, perspectives, and ideas that don't conform with our mental models, even if they're true.

It's the same reason why I ignored the benefits of social media and started using platforms like Facebook less; my mental model prevented me from noticing and appreciating the benefits of social media, instead focusing on its downsides.

Ultimately, failing to account for your or others' mental models when trying to instigate a behavior change will undoubtedly lead to friction and frustration.

What's perhaps most perplexing about small farms struggling is there are established methods, treatments, and tools addressing specific challenges they face, but farmers are reluctant to adopt them. It's crucial they innovate and optimize to compete, but their ingrained ways of thinking limit their chances to learn from professional guidance and implement novel ideas. Their hesitation to change their ways—which is completely understandable given how difficult it is for anyone to do so—is one reason why they may lose to agribusinesses and give up farming entirely.

The key to saving small farms lies in communicating necessary interventions and expert advice matching farmers' mental models. Agricultural educators need to introduce new information and ideas in ways that acknowledge farmers' mental models and highlight similarities between them. If they can listen and address the problems they're facing, there's hope yet for the survival of small farms that are the backbone of America.

CHRYSLER'S MILLION VEHICLE RECALL

"Good design goes to heaven; bad design goes everywhere."
—*Mieke Gerritzen*

Interaction design is a complex field, but at its heart lies a quest to find the best possible match between the user's mental model and the conceptual model being presented to them with any product or service.

In his seminal book, *The Design of Everyday Things*, Donald Norman popularized the term "mental models" by describing how a system is designed and implemented on the basis of the designer's way of thinking.

Norman postulated that, regardless of what product or service is at play, individuals develop a mental model of how they think a system works through their interactions. This internal representation is used to reason about the system, anticipate system behavior, and explain why the system reacts the way it does. While Norman's definition of mental models is more systems focused, it overlaps with our understanding that there are patterns in our minds representing how we think things work.

Here are a few examples of mental models at play—in terms of interaction design—in everyday situations and tasks:

- **Booking a flight:** You have a basic expectation of what steps you will take, such as entering your personal information, choosing a seat, and paying for it. You also expect to be informed whether there's an extra fee for baggage or if it's included.
- **Cooking on a stove:** You expect the positioning of the burner dials matches the orientation of the burners. In other words, you'd anticipate the left-most burner dial would control the left-most burner.
- **Using a chat app like WhatsApp or Facebook Messenger:** You expect messages will go back and forth in real time, and you can also send attachments like photos and GIFs. You expect to be notified as soon as someone has replied to you.

- **Washing your hands in the bathroom:** You expect cold water would come out after turning the right handle and hot water would come out when turning the left handle. You also know the degree you turn the handle corresponds to water pressure, meaning slightly turning either handle would result in a lower volume of water being dispensed versus turning either handle more.
- **Driving a car:** You have expectations of what the main things you can interact with are, what the car is capable of, and how to appropriately drive it in your country, such as what side of the road to be on. You'd expect shifting the car to park means moving the gearshift all the way to the top and leaving it there.

What's common in these cases is that mental models we've unconsciously constructed guide our behavior and help us navigate simple and complex tasks.

When we encounter novel situations, like using a bathroom at a friend's place we've never been to or driving a new car model, we minimize our cognitive load by applying familiar ways of thinking to guide us.

Mental models encapsulate the beliefs a user holds about any given system or interactions with them. In most instances, the belief will, to a certain extent, resemble the real-life model.

This is important because users will plan and predict future actions within a system based on their mental models. Designers can tap into users' mental models so their products successfully communicate their function through their form.

But it only works if they take the time to understand their users' mental models. It is an all-too-common failing of designs to be based on their creators' mental models, which are often too different or detailed to bear any relationship with a user's way of thinking.

And sometimes these designs, disconnected from ubiquitous mental models, have unintended but deadly consequences.

The last thing any automaker wants is a recall, especially after releasing vehicles they've spent years developing and millions to make.

Unfortunately, that's exactly the position Chrysler found themselves in 2016 after the injuries kept piling up, leading to an astounding 1.1 million recalls and the death of beloved *Star Trek* actor, Anton Yelchin (Ramey 2016).

Unlike most recalls, this one didn't occur because a core part of the vehicle was malfunctioning; in this case, drivers who operated their vehicles faithful to the Chrysler team's intent found themselves in scary situations.

Why, you ask?

All thanks to a mental model mismatch with the new electronic shifter they implemented in several of their recent car models.

Specifically, the 2012-2014 Dodge Chargers, Chrysler 300 sedans, and 2014-2015 Jeep Grand Cherokee SUVs were unlike their predecessors in a dangerous way: the shifter design made it difficult to tell which gear the vehicle was in (Ramey 2016).

Most shifters use positional feedback, along with symbols marking each gear, to easily indicate whether you're in park, reverse, neutral, or drive. These visual cues align with our ingrained way of thinking and the beliefs informed by them, which is why this new design created a lot of friction.

Nilay Patel, reporter for popular technology news website *The Verge*, sat in one of the recalled vehicles sharing that "it is really confusing. It's a weird mix of software and hardware that doesn't quite work the way you expect." The shifter design, appropriately named the Monostable shifter, was extremely confusing. With traditional shifters, when you change the gear from park to drive, the shifter changes position and a visual symbol lights up to indicate the current gear. But with the Monostable shifter, after moving the shifter to the desired gear, it would return to the center position, making it unclear what gear the vehicle was in.

To completely confirm if you're in drive or park or reverse, you have to look at either the LEDs on the shifter (often covered by your palm) or the digital display in the instrument cluster. If that wasn't bad enough, the usual "click" we hear when the gear shifts was muted in this design—exacerbating the existing confusion.

Ultimately the National Highway Traffic Safety Administration concluded that "operation of the Monostable shifter is not intuitive and provides poor tactile and visual feedback to the driver, increasing the potential for unintended gear selection" (Ramey 2016).

Naturally, this was confusing to drivers who, upon returning to the parking lot, discovered in horror the car they believed they had safely parked was rolling away.

Of course, hindsight is always 20/20, but in this case, the Chrysler team's foresight was 20/30.

By mid-April of 2016, the automaker reported seven hundred incidents of vehicles rolling away after intending to shift to park in the 2014–2015 Grand Cherokee, resulting in 212 crashes (Jensen 2016). Forty-one of those caused injuries, including Anton Yelchin's untimely death (Jensen 2016).

Anton Yelchin, just twenty-seven, was well-known for playing Chekov in the rebooted *Star Trek* series but passed away after his 2015 Jeep Grand Cherokee pinned him against a mailbox pillar at his home in Los Angeles (Jensen 2016).

Challenging existing mental models causes friction and requires discipline, experience, and accountability to successfully shift. Chrysler should take a page out of Donald Norman's book to ensure subsequent designs fit users' mental models instead of causing friction and confusion by upending them.

ECUADOR'S FAILED "TODOS SOMOS MESTIZOS" CAMPAIGN

"I think color blindness is a noble idea, but so are unicorns and tooth fairies. The data show that it is simply a misleading and, indeed, harmful way to frame how race plays out in today's society."
—*Osagie K. Obasogie*

"I don't see color" is one of the most frustrating phrases ever uttered. Unfortunately, it's one of the go-to responses those with privilege use to address concerns around unconscious bias and racism, but it's nonsensical.

After all, as Trevor Noah once quipped, "So what do you do at a traffic light?" How can we claim to be antiracist if we don't even acknowledge that race is a critical part of people's identities and cannot just be ignored?

Attempting to be color-blind simply blinds us to the real issues at hand. That's exactly the lesson Ecuador's government learned the hard way when it began its "Todos Somos Mestizos" program. Implemented in the 1930s, this initiative roughly translates to "we are all mixed race."

At the time, the government of Guillermo Rodríguez Lara espoused the ideology that "we all are mestizo" throughout Ecuador to curb the racism which sharply divided the country. These efforts manifested in behaviors like omitting asking for one's racial or ethnic identity through national censuses (Chávez 2017).

While this ideology and those actions were noble-minded, the government completely ignored how deeply embedded racism had become due to Ecuadorians' ingrained ways of thinking. The program failed spectacularly because of it.

According to World Population Review, in 2014, Ecuador's population roughly comprised of Mestizos (71.9 percent), Amerindians (7 percent), Afro-Ecuadorians (7 percent), and Whites (12.1 percent). Despite this rich diversity, the Whites and Mestizos have oppressed Amerindians and Afro-Ecuadorians for years.

Andres Chavez, researcher at the Universidad Internacional del Ecuador, studied why Ecuador's racism problem persisted despite the country's diversity and initiatives like "Todos Somos Mestizos."

He and his team acknowledge the paradox of Ecuador's racism problem, mentioning that "Ecuador is home to people of every skin color that can be found in the world. Despite this racial diversity, racism is a prevalent problem in the country. This problem is so deeply rooted in society that many Ecuadorians are unaware of it" (Chávez 2017).

As we've examined previously, the mechanisms invisibly influencing Ecuadorians were their mental models. The deadly confluence of sociological norms, Eurocentric power structures, and decades of enforced racial hierarchies subtly shaped their patterns of thinking.

Even to the point they largely aren't even aware of what racism, discrimination, and prejudice are. In fact, Whites, the group with the highest rate of awareness, only scored 55 percent, 41 percent, and 34 percent in knowledge of racism, discrimination, and prejudice (Chávez 2017).

To be clear, this is very different than trying to be color-blind. In this case, the individuals at hand don't even have a vocabulary to discuss the issues to which that phrase even refers.

The lack of awareness and discussion of these problems is a huge stumbling block to making any material difference; it simply reinforces the existing ways of thinking in a vicious cycle.

There has never been a segregation law in Ecuador, but "because Indians are seen as 'inferior,' they have to go to the back of the bus in order not to inconvenience their White and Mestizo 'superiors'" (Chávez 2017).

That racist thoughts and attitudes are reinforced through invisible systems of power make these experiences seem so common and natural that Ecuadorians do not recognize them as products of racism.

Paola Betchart, a Mestiza education and outreach advocate now living in the United States, recalled common experiences of racism growing up in Ecuador in the 1980s: "The government had a whitewashing crusade to homogenize the population and sell the idea that everyone is Mestizo. But in the practical experience of life when you'd go to the store and there were two people at the counter everyone knew the person who was Whiter would be served first."

Paola's experience reveals just how difficult and futile it is to shift ingrained patterns of thinking and understanding of the way the world works. Even as of 2017, a significant racial issue in Ecuadorian society is the desire to become whiter or to improve one's race.

One of the main concerns for a family when a baby is born is what their skin color will be. An Ecuadorian man recounted how, after visiting his cousin's light-skinned baby, one of his political relatives commented, "It is great, the race has been improved" (Chávez 2017).

This is not only an issue for the Amerindian and Afro-Ecuadorian population. The general consensus in Ecuador is that "the Indian wants to be a Mestizo, the Mestizo wishes to be white, and the White yearns to be a gringo" (Chávez 2017).

There is a clear social issue in the mental models of Ecuadorians in which each person desires to be at least a little bit Whiter. It's striking how prevalent this pattern of thinking is, but it shouldn't come as a surprise, given the country's history of oppression by White people. As we saw with the injuries Chrysler's new shifter design caused, this program was doomed to fail because it didn't align with people's mental models.

Unfortunately, until racism, discrimination, and prejudice are recognized as real issues, little can be done to change the way people of different ethnic groups see and treat each other and themselves.

We can't make racism disappear by washing people's identities away; it's impossible to notice physiological differences in one another and activate familiar mental models reinforcing racial hierarchies. Racism in Ecuador has so deeply permeated society that it unofficially dictates where people can live, and those with darker skin who stray outside of these regions face even more prejudice.

The first step to address this problem is to educate people of all ethnic groups about racism and its consequences, and then to take action to unlearn mental models reinforcing notions of caste and racial hierarchies and create new pathways of thinking.

Dismantling those hierarchies and Eurocentric thinking, which celebrates Whiteness and denounces darkness, is no easy task. But the journey is a lot clearer with mental models in mind. Instead of ignoring them, every effort must be made to unlearn and shift destructive patterns of thinking.

So, what do saving small farms, Chrysler's massive recall, and Ecuador's failed whitewashing campaign all have in common? They illustrate how understanding mental models is crucial to changing or achieving a desired behavior. We need to understand others' patterns of thinking and tailor suggestions, changes, and solutions to fit their mental models, or they'll be rejected. It's equally important to unravel what's driving the mental model and reach the primary source to mitigate its cascading effects—like how two hundred years of Spanish rule and reinforced caste identities caused Ecuadorians to associate White skin tones with superiority even after the Spanish left.

Those passionate about saving small farms, which are reluctant to make changes necessary to survive in an increasingly competitive world, must recommend solutions with farmers' ways of thinking in mind. If automakers make an integral part of the car work in a way that doesn't match people's mental models, there needs to be additional cues or guard-rails to account for the inevitable friction. Ecuador and other nations that try to erase racism without acknowledging it exists and is reinforced by sticky mental models shouldn't expect any outcome other than failure.

If applying a mental model perspective to situations others have experienced is enlightening, how might mental models help us in our daily lives?

Change—Rohit Gupta

Change is challenging yourself,

inviting

and embracing discomfort,

pushing past fear,
and shedding many tears.

Change is a journey,

lonely

yet fulfilling.

Change is chasing perfection,

knowing

it's unobtainable,
but proceeding regardless.

Change is questioning values,

asking

why repeatedly,
and never being satisfied with easy answers.

Change is a truth of nature,

impermanence

is the very nature
of things.

Change is the fruit of hard labor,

invisible

to all
but observable when in motion.

Change is to know the real self,

unburdened

by patterns of thinking.

Change is a shift in mindset,

within

our grasp,
if we so choose.

REFLECTIONS

- What are three examples of poor design (in terms of failing to align with mental models) you've noticed in your life? Focus on physical or digital products and experiences, like a remote or a registration workflow for an app.
- Some Tesla models enable gear shifting through the center touchscreen console and have done away with physical controls. Does this concern you from a mental model lens? Why?
- How can you leverage mental models to induce a positive behavior change at work, with family and friends, or with your partner?
- Recall a time when you struggled to convince someone to make a positive change in their life. If you could go back in time, would you approach that conversation differently with an understanding of their ingrained ways of thinking?
- Why does the success of any desired change, at a personal level, require understanding the mental models at play? Is any long-lasting change possible without shifting ways of thinking?

EXERCISES

- Practice seeing things from someone else's way of thinking by following the steps below.
  - Step one: Think about a conflict you're having. What is it about? Who is it with? How do you feel about it? What steps do you want to take? Take a few minutes to write down your answers to the previous questions.

This can help you process your thoughts and emotions better. Before moving on to the next step, really try to understand the underlying the conflict you're experiencing.

- Step two: Think about what's bothering you from the perspective of the person(s) you're having the conflict with. How do you think they see the conflict? How do you think they feel about it, and why do you think they feel that way? What were their intentions? Take a few minutes to write about the conflict from the other person(s) perspective.
- Step three: Return to your own perspective. Answer the questions from step one again. Did this help you to think about the conflict in a different way? Are your answers to the questions the same as before, or have they changed?

• Imagine that instead of implementing the "Todos Somos Mestizos" program, the Ecuadorian government tapped you to address the rampant problem of racism. What are three strategies you would recommend to shift the public's ingrained way of thinking? How would you measure the success of those strategies?

Why Apply

"We are all stuck in this loop called life,
doing the same thing over and again."

—BHUVAN MOHANAN

Did you hear about the computer programmer who died in the shower?

He dutifully followed the instructions on his shampoo bottle: 'Lather, rinse, repeat.'

While that never actually happened (at least I hope not), we're all a bit like that programmer: once we activate and continue using a thinking pattern, we become stuck in an endless loop, doomed to think, act, and follow.

Some of these patterns, of which we're not consciously aware, include deeply ingrained caste notions, racial stereotypes, and the tendency to blame a lack of effort for failing to change our behavior.

The key benefit of applying a mental model lens—viewing things as ingrained patterns of thinking—to our lives is understanding how harmful loops originate and illuminating what we can do to break them.

WHY UNLEARNING IS SO DIFFICULT

"I've often heard people give very eloquent discussions on principles and ideals but many of them are still in trouble themselves. They are unable to escape from habit patterns and from the traditional backgrounds from which we have all come in one way or another."
—*Manly P. Hall*

People always say you never forget how to ride a bike, but what do you do if you actually want to?

Destin Sandlin, a missile flight testing engineer living in Huntsville, Alabama, didn't realize it at the time, but he'd be the first person to answer that question. It all started one day when his friend, Barney, called him out of the blue.

You see, where Destin worked, the US Army Test & Evaluation Command Center, his welding coworkers were geniuses who loved pranking the engineers. One day, Barney, a gifted welder, presented Destin with a challenge that seemed simple enough: ride a bike without falling. Easy, right?

From the outside, Barney's bike looked like any other two-wheeler, but it was modified in one small, game-changing way: the handlebars worked in reverse. When you turned the handlebar to the left, the wheel went to the right. When you turned it to the right, the wheel went to the left. Sounds frustrating, huh?

Destin, always up for a challenge, jumped on the bike ready to prove how quickly he could conquer this. Within five seconds, Destin found himself lying on the floor. After several more attempts, he realized this was a really difficult task. No matter what he tried—thinking deeply about how the handles were reversed, pedaling faster, or turning the handle in reverse direction before pedaling—he couldn't succeed.

If we never forget how to ride a bike, why was operating one with a single modification proving so difficult? Now, I know what you're probably thinking: Destin is just an uncoordinated engineer that couldn't do it. But that's not the case at all.

Consider how difficult the algorithm associated with riding a bike is from a physics perspective: you have to account for downward force on the pedals, lean your whole body, pull and push the handlebars, account for gyroscopic procession in the wheels, manage tension in the tires supporting your weight, shift anywhere from three to thirty gears, and leverage friction brakes turning energy to heat. How in the world do we remember how to do all that—without thinking about it—once we learn?

If you've been paying attention, you'll know the answer is once again our mental models. Turns out that once we learn how to ride a bike, we don't forget because it's stored in a thought pattern—how a bike works—that we use so proficiently and frequently it becomes second nature, like breathing.

You'll notice similar, effortless behavior in what we consider "muscle memory," an ability we see demonstrated whenever we play musical instruments after long breaks, carry out common body movements such as typing, or even simply drive a car. Once mental models are formed and reinforced, though, they become very difficult to change. In fact, unlearning these kinds of automatic behaviors might be the most difficult given it's harder to catch oneself when it happens.

Coming back to Destin, after failing miserably to ride the special bike, he set out on a journey to understand why this was so hard. He wanted to show others they couldn't do it as well. So, whenever he spoke at universities and conferences (fairly often for someone with a PhD in Aerospace Engineering), he took the special bike with him. But it was always the same result. People thought they could power through it or somehow trick their brain, but it never worked.

Somehow, after eight months of practicing daily, many wrecks, and countless jokes from his neighbors, Destin finally did it.

He remarked in his viral YouTube video *The Backwards Brain Bicycle* that:

> *One day I couldn't ride the bike, and the next day I could. It was like I could feel like some kind of pathway in my brain that was now unlocked. It was really weird though. It's like there's a trail in my brain, but if I wasn't paying close enough attention to it, my brain would easily lose that neural path and jump back onto the old road it was*

more familiar with. Any small distractions at all, like a cellphone ringing in my pocket, would instantly throw my brain back to the old control algorithm and I would wreck. But at least I could ride it.

With the experiment over, Destin wondered if he could still ride a regular bike. Sadly, in the crowded streets of Amsterdam, he quickly realized he no longer could, but after twenty minutes of fumbling around and making a fool of himself, suddenly his brain clicked back into the old algorithm.

Think about that for a second. It took him *eight months* to shift his mental model, and only *twenty minutes* to reactivate his old one. Destin's journey unlearning and then re-learning how to ride a bike illustrates just how difficult it is to take a fork in the road and avoid bumping into our past mental models. And if it took eight months of daily effort to unlearn a mental model most of us don't use frequently, just how hard would it be to unlearn patterns of thinking we unknowingly utilize often—like our caste identity?

You can take the Indian out of India, but you can't take the India out of the Indian. Or so it seems. New data and stories suggest hundreds of Indian-Americans struggle to relinquish the grip that ingrained caste values and associated notions of superiority or inferiority have on them.

Take Cisco's high profile caste discrimination case for example. In October of 2020, a group of Cisco engineers on an all-Indian work team filed a discrimination lawsuit against their dominant caste bosses who, according to them, had found out about an employee's caste status, discriminated against him, and retaliated when he complained to HR.

One of the oldest and most rigidly defined social hierarchies in the world, India's caste system was formed more than three thousand years ago. Isabel Wilkerson, in her beautifully written book *Caste*, defines a caste as the "granting or withholding of respect, status, honor, attention, privileged resources, benefit of the doubt, and human kindness to someone based on their perceived rank." Originally, the caste system divided society into four main groups, with each division representing a social status and a generalized profession.

These castes in descending order of status are: **Brahmins** (the priestly and scholarly caste who provide for the intellectual and spiritual needs of the ruler and community), **Kshatriyas** (the ruler and warrior caste who rule and protect others), **Vaishyas** (the merchant and landowning caste designed to look after commerce and agriculture), and **Shudras** (the manual labor and service provider caste). But in the past few hundred years, a fifth group was formed for those carrying out very menial and polluting work having to do with bodily decay and dirt: **Dalits**. As this group exists outside of the caste system and are generally excluded from mainstream society, its members are labelled "outcasts."

While the power of the caste system seems to be waning, those born into lower castes still face significant hardships in their personal and professional lives. An Indian engineer, using the alias "Sam Cornelius" due to fears for his safety, came regularly to the United States from India since the mid-nineties. He's worked as an IT contractor at several companies, including the tech giant Cisco.

From the beginning, he loved living in the US. Here, no one knew what caste he was, and most weren't familiar with India's caste system, which was extremely liberating as Sam was born a Dalit, commonly known as Untouchables. For centuries, Dalits have been relegated to the filthiest and most demeaning jobs in society, like removing dead carcasses from the road, clearing public latrines by hand, and collecting garbage.

Unfortunately, Dalits continue to be treated like they're worthless and spiritually unclean. NPR reports that "Dalit women are raped more than women of other castes. Dalit men get lynched for falling in love with dominant caste women" (NPR 2020). Growing up, Sam shared, he would hear anti-Dalit insults on the sports field. He wasn't welcome in everyone's homes either. Liberated from the shackles of his socially constructed caste identity, Sam felt equal to others for the first time in his life in the US.

When Sam Cornelius's American coworkers asked him about India and his life there, you can imagine what a relief it was that they didn't ask him about his caste—neither directly nor inadvertently. Much like racism in the United States, the Indian caste system is deeply rooted and systemic in nature, persisting through inherited beliefs, cultural and class identity, and institutional inequity even after legal discrimination was abolished. When he left India, Sam thought he left these antiquated, harmful beliefs behind.

But that sadly wasn't the case. According to the lawsuit, he was allegedly "expected to accept a caste hierarchy within the workplace where [he] held the lowest status within the team, and, as a result, received less pay, fewer opportunities, and other inferior terms and conditions of employment" (NPR 2020). When Sam opposed his treatment, the senior leadership on his team retaliated against him by "reducing his role on the team, isolating him from colleagues and giving him assignments that were impossible to complete under the circumstances" (NPR 2020).

You might be wondering how they figured out Sam's caste. They'd try to tease it out by asking pointed questions about his surname, hometown, and even his diet. For instance, some people may harmlessly ask an Indian if they're vegetarian because Brahmins are well known to be strict vegetarians. But if you are Indian intent on finding out another Indian's caste, you'd ask something like, "Are you vegetarian by birth or by choice?"

While the attention the Cisco lawsuit received is certainly encouraging, no legal action has been taken as of early 2022. To make matters worse, cases like Sam's are becoming more and more common. Dalit activist, Thenmozhi Soundararajan, runs the human rights group Equality Labs, which hosted a virtual town hall following the lawsuit.

Soundararajan mentioned that, in response to a survey, her group received more than three hundred complaints from other South Asians reporting caste discrimination in the US tech sector (NPR 2020). Previous research confirms the prevalence of caste-related discrimination as well. A 2018 survey of 1,200 individuals of South Asian descent in the United States found that 26 percent of respondents experienced physical assault because of their caste, while 59 percent reported caste-based derogatory jokes or remarks directed at them. More than half said they were afraid of being outed as Dalits (Ray 2019). While this survey was conducted anonymously and likely had a disproportionate number of Dalits respond, it underscores the surprising frequency of overt caste discrimination within the Indian-American community.

And just a year after Cisco's caste case, a lawsuit alleged that Bochasanwasi Shri Akshar Purushottam Swaminarayan Sanstha, a Hindu religious group, lured over two hundred lower-caste workers to New Jersey to build a temple while being paid little over a dollar and twenty cents (Krishnan 2021). To be fair, much of the overt racism is perpetrated by first-generation Indian immigrants as the religious group's awful treatment of lower-caste workers confirms.

In fact, a study by the Carnegie Endowment for International Peace found that:

Roughly half of all Hindu Indian-Americans identify with a caste group. Foreign-born respondents are significantly more likely than US-born respondents to espouse a caste identity. The overwhelming majority of Hindus with a caste identity—more than eight in ten—self-identify as belonging to the category of General or upper caste (Badrinathan et al. 2021).

My belief is far more Indian-Americans—regardless of being born in India or America—possess a caste identity manifesting in more subtle, disguised ways. As someone born a Vaishya, and proud of it, I've been taught Brahmins are usually smart, and it would be great to marry one of them. But the worst thing imaginable would be to marry someone born into a lower caste. Other Indian-American friends report having to pass a "caste test," confirming they belong to an upper caste as well, when meeting their partner's parents for the first time.

That caste discrimination and caste identities, uniquely Indian inventions, are so rampant in America speaks to just how difficult it is to unlearn ingrained patterns of thinking. But considering Black people have been treated like Dalits in the United States for decades—and continue to be despite a long struggle for equality—maybe it isn't so surprising after all. It's no coincidence that Martin Luther King Jr. once declared, "Yes, I am an untouchable, and every negro in the United States of America is an untouchable" (Wilkerson 2020).

Sam and Destin's stories make it seem like unlearning is difficult for everyday folks like you and me, but you'd imagine that people who've undergone rigorous scientific training (who make decisions based on data, not beliefs) should be better at it. Right?

Seventeen years is an incredible amount of time. It represents the journey we all take from birth to reaching the doorstep of adulthood. But seventeen years represents something else incredible: the time it takes for a research idea to be implemented in clinical practice (Niven 2017). If it takes seventeen years to implement a new idea, by that same logic discarding outdated practices must take several years as well.

If you knew there was research available to improve the care you required, wouldn't you want your healthcare provider to use that research to inform decisions pertaining to your care? Wouldn't you want to receive care scientifically proven to be beneficial?

For example, cervical cancer screening for women under the age of thirty doesn't help and causes unnecessary follow-up testing (Rosenberg et al. 2015). We now know the use of bone cement to treat painful spine fractures among patients with osteoporosis does not improve pain (Buchbinder et al. 2019). It turns out the placement of stents in patients with narrowed arteries is no better than treatment with medications alone (Boden et al. 2017). Although recent research demonstrates each of these interventions do not improve patient outcomes, they persist in current clinical practice.

Maybe scientifically trained folks aren't any better than the rest of us at unlearning after all. It's universally difficult. The truthfully proverbial seventeen-year time lag from clinical idea to actual adoption, which encapsulates the political, bureaucratic, and risk averse challenges inherent in healthcare as well, illustrates how hard unlearning can be, even for the most data driven among us. It's no coincidence phrases like "creature of habit" and "resistance to change" are widely used to describe humans in general and physicians in particular.

To this day, it befuddles me how, despite the obvious benefits, it took office-based physicians over forty years to reach an 86 percent adoption rate of electronic health records or EHRs (HealthIT.gov 2017). EHRs are well documented to improve the quality of care, reduce medical errors, boost patient satisfaction, and sharpen financial and operational performance. They even play a crucial role in conducting population-level health studies.

Even discounting the relatively high cost of computers in the '80s and '90s, the slow adoption of EHRs amongst doctors begs a larger question: is their difficulty unlearning due to a lack of effort or our fundamental human nature? That doctors have trouble learning is a flashing red neon sign that mental models are at play. After all, these amazing individuals are driven by fact and science; that's why we don't see them handing out herbal remedies they hear about from friends or Instagram ads. They should be adept at changing perspective in response to new data, which literally is the idea behind the scientific method, right?

My genius sister and now Stanford trained oncologist, Divya Gupta, and a team of Case Western University faculty were puzzled by these findings as well. She and her team studied a group of fifteen primary care physicians—of different ages and clinical experience practicing at the Cleveland Veterans Affair Medical Center—to elucidate the unlearning that takes place at a physician level. What they found might surprise you.

But before we dive into the results of their study, let's take a moment to appreciate what unlearning entails. Merriam-Webster defines unlearning as "putting out of one's knowledge or memory or discarding the habit of." Although this concept can be defined in many ways, a strikingly poignant one is Karen Becker's definition of unlearning: "the process by which individuals and organizations acknowledge and release prior learning (including assumptions and mental frameworks) in order to incorporate new information and behaviors" (Becker 2005).

I find Becker's definition helpful because it highlights the most difficult aspect of unlearning: letting go of our mental models. As we've explored, mental models can be very difficult to shift once they've been ingrained, whether they're notions of caste or the algorithm for how to ride a bike. What's fascinating about mental models is they can transform associations and beliefs into truths guiding how we interact with our world. Everyone is susceptible to this—even doctors.

My sister's and her team's goal was to understand the experience of abandoning outdated clinical practices and ways of thinking and examine how that impedes or accelerates learning new practices. By doing so, they aimed to inform more successful phasing out of ineffective clinical practices. The team gathered data through thirty-minute in-person, qualitative interviews at the VA medical center asking questions about physicians' clinical practices and how they've adapted to changes over time.

When a change is introduced, whether through the introduction of new guidelines or self-initiated, physicians face various struggles to successfully change practice and reach a new equilibrium. One set of these struggles includes those related to the change itself, such as the ease of implementation or inherent discomfort with the change. Physician Two, referring to new cholesterol guidelines, describes it as follows:

Their whole background of thinking—this whole idea of not treating to a number. I think we like to have finite goals and endpoints, which some will argue we still have that, now we're just treating to a goal dose instead of a goal LDL. I think it's good to treat a patient and not a number, so that's fine. It's still a shift in paradigm. Many changes not only challenge old habits but also require a shift in paradigm regarding a physician's approach to the practice, resulting in even more of a struggle in adopting the change (Gupta et al. 2017).

The paradigm shift—focusing on holistic treatment of cholesterol instead of a target number—is uniquely difficult because it challenges existing mental models deeply ingrained. Even if this change makes logical sense, changing one's pattern of thinking and then their behavior is another story entirely.

The nature of the change itself also affects the ease of unlearning. For instance, a change requiring an addition is perceived to be easier than a change requiring the cessation of a current practice; it's easier to expand an existing mental model than it is to change one. Physician Three in the study poignantly stated:

It's easier to introduce something new than to take out something old. Bringing in a new drug, a new pill to people and telling them that this has showed good evidence, people will introduce it right away, it will be on formulary in two weeks and physicians will be prescribing it left and right. Telling people to stop doing something is almost close to impossible. It takes so many years, it takes so many changes, it takes so many events, and it still doesn't happen in 100 percent of the people (Gupta et al. 2017).

Why is it so much harder to unlearn than learn? Mental models are the key insight here. Unlearning requires overcoming established patterns of thinking rooted in assumption, belief, and experiences shaping our very understanding of things. For instance, if something we've been doing is revealed to be harmful, but we have experiences contradicting that, why would we change tactics now? There's no need to fix something that isn't broken, and it's easy to make excuses.

We can see that attitude present in anti-vaxxers who refuse to be vaccinated on the grounds that they aren't at risk, despite going about their lives normally. Or in frequent cocaine users who know how harmful the substance is but keep doing it because they've been fine so far. Or in dieters who excuse having unhealthy snacks because they're just one-off incidents. In all these cases, over indexing on our experiences and exposures results in problematic mental models that can be difficult to change.

Doctors are no different.

Physician Five, who is at one end of the evidence-based medicine spectrum, confirms:

How you take up a revised recommendation depends heavily on your personal experience and your personal biases, how you interpret literature. And I think this is how it works for everybody. We all have a mouthful with evidence-based medicine, but very few of us are truly evidence-based. Most of us are like a snippet-based, based off what you hear, what you read, what other people explain to you, what a mentor or somebody you really respect says. It's a mixture (Gupta et al. 2017).

Physician Five reveals adopting a new practice really depends on your mental model, influenced by what we hear, our peers, and our own experiences, much more so than the physical data at hand. Physicians, like the rest of us, are surrounded by many sources of information including classical evidence consisting of published literature, but also unstructured sources of data, such as conversations with colleagues and personal clinical experience. These inputs assist physicians in making clinical decisions both grounded in data and practical experience.

The same individual admitted to prescribing hormone replacement therapy (HRT), basically injecting estrogen, to patients dealing with menopause symptoms like hot flashes, despite studies clearly showing that doing so increases breast cancer risks (McNulty 2020).

My sister, Dr. Gupta, noted in our conversation:

When a woman enters menopause, their ovaries stop producing estrogen. So as a result, they go through a lot of symptoms in response to a lack of estrogen in their body: hot flashes, changes in their skin, dryness. And they're really uncomfortable. I want to say that until the mid-2000s women were being regularly prescribed estrogen or hormone replacement therapy (HRT). It sounds pretty benign, right? Your ovaries aren't producing estrogen, so let's just replace that to alleviate symptoms. But it turns out that cancer, especially breast cancer, is driven by estrogen. So, women who were receiving hormone therapy were developing breast cancer. Estrogen also increased clotting risks, and they were developing blood clots. Ultimately hormone replacement therapy fell out of favor because of its adverse effects.

Unfortunately, Physician Five continued prescribing hormone replacement therapy to her patients.

In the end, on a population level, the heavy use of HRT probably did cause some problems, but for me as an individual, I probably didn't have a single patient in my practice who got breast cancer from HRT, right. So, this is sort of the disconnect you have between population management and the few 100 patients I saw (Gupta et al. 2017).

The physician's lack of personal experience with the adverse effects of HRT and respect for patient autonomy drove her to continue prescribing estrogen therapy for those who desired it. It's an interesting example of how data can nudge individuals to act a certain way, but ultimately couldn't override the existing mental model.

Unlearning is uniquely challenging because it requires shifting mental models. As we saw with Destin earlier, it is possible to unlearn how to ride a bike but doing so involves a ton of time and focus. The first step is acknowledging the role mental models play, and the next step is to shift them, which we'll discuss further on in the book.

UNRAVELING UNCONSCIOUS BIAS

"Human beings are poor examiners, subject to superstition, bias, prejudice, and a PROFOUND tendency to see what they want to see rather than what is really there."

—M. Scott Peck

Every human being has unconscious bias. Even the most progressive, virtuous advocates for equality—even Nelson Mandela.

The insidious power and persistence of mental models manifesting in unconscious bias is strikingly captured by a story Nelson Mandela told of a time when he flew from Sudan to Ethiopia. He started to worry when he noticed the pilot was Black:

> *We put down briefly in Khartoum, where we changed to an Ethiopian Airways flight to Addis. Here I experienced a rather strange sensation. As I was boarding the plane, I saw that the pilot was Black. I had never seen a Black pilot before, and the instant I did I had to quell my panic. How could a Black man fly an airplane? But a moment later I caught myself: I had fallen into the apartheid mindset, thinking Africans were inferior and that flying was a White man's job (Segal 2004).*

Despite being an anti-apartheid revolutionary, even Nelson Mandela's unconscious, involuntary response to seeing a Black pilot was to worry. This isn't a knock on Mandela, but rather it poignantly illustrates how deeply embedded racism and notions of caste are.

Even individuals like Mandela, whose missions are to counteract notions of caste, are susceptible to ideological influences encoding the stereotypes around treating people of different castes. Bias isn't something we can simply unlearn—it's something we must train ourselves to be aware of and take steps to mitigate when harmful.

Mental models are at play here as they are responsible for constructing internal representations of caste order, explaining why Mandela exhibited an automatic, reflexive response to seeing a Black pilot. Similar to bias, mental models aren't something we can just get rid of. Nor should we. Instead, we should strive to be aware of them, minimizing their negative influence while optimizing their positive benefits.

Taking a step back, recall that mental models fundamentally organize how we pay attention—whether we accept or reject evidence or experiences in relation to concepts we develop a model around. They also inform how we respond to different stimuli and shape the reactions and conclusions we draw as the example of Nelson Mandela painfully illustrates.

Perhaps the many forms of unfair discrimination—racism, sexism, ableism, transphobia, etc.—are all rooted within faulty mental models shaped by prevailing ideologies and sociocultural attitudes resulting in worry, anger, or discomfort when the expectations of reality we form are challenged by contradictory evidence. Failing to acknowledge the sources of those internal thought patterns risks turning them into external realities when we're confronted by situations that cause friction with our mental models.

Depending on one's upbringing and experiences, this may include phenomena like boarding a plane with a Black pilot, working at a company with a female executive, encountering a disabled person in the physical spaces one dwells, and seeing a transgender individual. In each of these cases, the situation at hand activates a particular mental model that, in some cases, is troubled by what is happening; should we expect people to feel or react differently when their entire perception of reality, shaped by their mental models, is confronted? Unfortunately, in a harmless attempt to minimize cognitive load, mental models are inherently structured in such a way that bias naturally forms based on the limitations of one's experiences and the beliefs they are immersed in.

We previously explored how mental models, in simplifying complex topics and subjects into preservable meanings and representations, reinforce beliefs and meanings gradually separated from the contexts that informed them. So, it's no surprise they often result in parochial perspectives. This is especially troublesome when the beliefs being reinforced are stereotypical or pejorative in nature.

While it's definitely an oversimplification, consider for a moment an individual who grew up surrounded by coded language and negative racial stereotypes that turns out to be unsurprisingly racist as an adult. What's perhaps most unfortunate about this is, to a large extent, the automatic response that individual exhibits when exposed to or thinking about members of a particular racial group is not the result of some traumatizing real-world experiences; the individual's mental model was shaped by their experiences and sociocultural contexts and persisted even though they weren't based on truth or fact.

Consider the example of Zack Arias: a White, cisgender man who grew up in Georgia's Gwinnett County during the late 1970s to 1980s, surrounded by kids who looked like him. Zack, who is forty-seven in 2022, recalls growing up surrounded by racial biases that many saw no issue with:

> *Family jokes riddled with slurs were appropriate as long as they were said behind closed doors, and teachers announced to kids their opposition to a referendum that would bring MARTA [a public transport operator in the Atlanta area] into Gwinnett because they said it would allow poor communities from Atlanta to bring more crime into the county (Kerns 2020).*

In the absence of other perspectives to inform his beliefs, Zack found himself getting angry and defensive toward other groups of people later in life. With the rise of the internet and social media that allowed groups from all over the world to finally connect, suddenly Zack had access to hear a diverse set of voices, but he had no desire to listen. The journalist who interviewed him shared that "[Zack] could count on one hand how many Black kids he may have come into contact with at school, and as a result of this 'white-washed' life, he was admittedly a racist for many, many years" (Kerns 2020).

Unfortunately, individuals may hold on to mental models that can have destructive consequences for their lives or the lives of others and may continue to use them to validate their interpretations, even when those models and interpretations are patently false. This is partly where the phenomena of confirmation bias originates as we interpret new information through our ever familiar mental models imparting us with an opposing sense of reality. Instead of looking for contradictory evidence, mental models tend to perceive information in a way consistent with the internal representation of the issue or topic at hand.

Imagine for a moment a hypothetical example in which Sally, who supports gun use, seeks out news stories and opinion pieces affirming her belief that gun ownership should not be limited. When she hears stories about shootings in the news, she interprets them in a way that confirms her existing beliefs; thinking mental health challenges are the real culprit here, not the tools being used. Or believing if everyone had guns, the shooter wouldn't have been as successful in carrying out his nefarious plot.

On the other hand, Henry is adamantly in favor of gun control. He searches for news sources and perspectives aligning with his thinking, and when he comes across stories about shootings, he interprets them as another example of how gun ownership must be restricted to ensure public safety.

Irrespective of where the truth in the issue lies, what's concerning is despite reading the same stories, Sally and Henry's pre-existing mental models shape the way they perceive the details, further confirming their beliefs. Unfortunately, over time we forget that mental models are, by nature, a simplification of our external reality. And before we know it, they become the default lens through which we perceive things. Mental models are why bias is unconscious and not something we're naturally aware of.

Mental models may also impart biases in decision making whenever we encounter situations requiring us to think or respond quickly, as Daniel Kahneman outlined in his book *Thinking Fast & Slow*. Kahneman explains that certain situations, such as those where limited time is available to make a decision and necessitate the ability to think and act quickly.

Unfortunately, over time our responses to these situations become codified into decision routines or heuristics executed automatically without us being aware of them and the information on which they are based. This automatic response is likely adaptive because it requires little demand on working memory while facilitating fast responses to situations that could be life-threatening. But it's important not to forget that context matters. Automatic responses proving useful in some situations can be harmful in others.

As an example of effective heuristics, math experts are fast and accurate in solving math problems because they have a much wider set of routines to apply, and these routines are developed to the point that they are applied automatically, without conscious effort. On the other hand, studies have shown that "people are quicker at categorizing threatening stimuli after seeing Black faces than after seeing White faces [when images are flashed on a monitor in a quick succession], which can result in the misidentification of harmless objects [such as toys] as weapons" (ScienceDaily 2016).

One of the main problems with using a mental model is, over time, it becomes the default way of explaining and understanding things, even if they aren't based on facts. While associating being overweight with being unhealthy may seem logical or even helpful, doing so subtly reinforces our unconscious beliefs in ways that can be harmful.

In this case, that mental model can tragically lead to body negativity and fat-shaming even though the belief underpinning it isn't accurate. The more we master a mental model, the more likely it is the mental model is applied indiscriminately without realizing it. In other words, if you have a hammer, everything looks like a nail. But recognizing there are multiple versions of the truth means relying on singular mental models is like cognitively restraining ourselves.

As another example, consider the question biologist Robert Sapolsky poses: "Why did the chicken cross the road?" Famously, Sapolsky provides different answers from different experts. An evolutionary biologist would contend the chicken crossed the road because they saw a potential mate on the other side, whereas a neuroscientist would argue the chicken acted in that way because the neurons in the chicken's brain fired and triggered the movement. Technically speaking, neither of these individuals is wrong, but nobody sees the entire picture. Each individual mental model merely comprises one view of reality.

The key to overcoming our bias is understanding how it's rooted in the unconscious formation and application of inaccurate mental models. Instead of answering why the chicken crossed the road from one perspective, we must endeavor to expose ourselves to other ways of thinking. We must offer several answers.

AVOID SELF-BLAME & REFRAME

"Losing weight is a mind game. Change your mind, change your body."

—*Author Unknown*

In the United States, we're taught from a young age that we're free to do whatever we'd like, and our destiny is very much in our own hands. Sounds empowering, huh? But the flipside of having this freedom and individual autonomy is if we're unable to accomplish our goals—like losing weight, breaking an addiction, or overcoming anxiety—there's no one to blame but ourselves. I used to think this way, and I don't fault others for believing so as well.

When I was an overweight teenager (I probably weighed 230 pounds when I was fourteen), I used to blame myself for the way I ate, looked, and felt. I'd internalized our society's message that I was fat because my willpower was weak, and I needed to work harder to change my unhealthy eating habits.

Naturally, that led me to look for easy ways out, which manifested in trying all sorts of diets, from paleo to keto and everything in between. Nothing worked. Yes, I'd lose a few pounds here and there, but the diets never really lasted because they weren't enjoyable, and I couldn't sustain the changes. It wasn't until my relationship with food had changed—no longer seeing food as a reward and exercise as a punishment—that I lost weight—and kept it off.

My experience losing weight coupled with an understanding of how difficult it is to change the way we perceive food makes me reconsider how I felt before. I wasn't overweight because of a lack of effort or desire; my ingrained patterns of thinking were responsible as well. In this case, my relationship with food, tendency to turn to it for comfort, and my food behavior—eating until I was stuffed and caving in to food cravings when I was stressed—were the real culprits.

And I'm not the only one who thinks this way. "Shifting your mindset about how to lose weight is the biggest factor in losing weight," says Kathryn Smerling, a therapist based in New York City (Howley 2021). She declares, "We can't shift our weight from the outside without realizing the correct inner resolve and intention" (Howley 2021).

Unfortunately, most people try to lose weight while in the worst state of mind possible: wanting to "fix" themselves. Similar to the journey I went through, many jump into diets and exercise plans when dismayed or disgusted with themselves, all the while pinching their "trouble" spots, calling themselves "fat" and feeling altogether less-than. And they get obsessed with results, focusing on quick fixes and losing sight of sustainability and even health.

"This type of thinking can be destructive," says Dr. Kevin Campbell, a cardiologist based in Raleigh, North Carolina (Howley 2021). "Rather than focusing on the good that can come of weight loss—such as better health, a longer life, more enjoyment in everyday activities and the prevention of diabetes and heart disease—these folks focus on negative thoughts. Ultimately, a negative mindset leads to failure" (Howley 2021).

Cultivating a mindset leading to success with weight loss is definitely difficult, but here are five ways to achieve it:

1. Practice mindful decision making.
2. Rethink rewards and punishments.
3. Identify your trouble thoughts.
4. Banish all-or-nothing thinking.
5. Lose the "foods are good or bad" mentality.

Psychologists stress that how you see yourself and your core identity—strongly shaped by our mental models—predicts your actions: see yourself as overweight, averse to exercise, or unworthy, and you'll act accordingly. Because our ingrained ways of thinking are the strongest predictors of how we think and act, our focus should be aligning them toward our goals instead of blindly applying more effort.

I noticed the same dynamic playing out with attitudes around addiction recovery.

"You have to want it" is a widespread myth that has evolved into an aphorism we accept without hesitation. The idea is addicts who are unable to get better—where better means seeking support, abstinence, and improved social functioning—simply aren't trying hard enough or secretly don't want to get better.

For the loved ones supporting addicts through their journey, until addicts prove they "want it," there's nothing those who care about them can do. Erin Stringfellow, a postdoctoral researcher studying drug use-related system dynamics, set out to understand this pervasive mental model of addiction recovery and its implications for sustaining change. In this context, mental models of addiction recovery are fundamentally about what it means to be an acceptable, worthy person in the eyes of modern capitalist society.

The fundamental thesis guiding the study was that people's mental models of addiction recovery, or their ingrained understanding of how addiction recovery works, affect the sustainability of interventions. Because mental models shape beliefs and actions, they have the potential to regulate or amplify change via feedback loops. Crucially, Dr. Stringfellow and her team realized that to understand a person's mental model is not to understand reality, but rather their view of reality. Those views, while understandable given one's experiences, can be more harmful than helpful.

Over the course of a few months, Dr. Stringfellow and her team interviewed fourteen drug users and ten of their loved ones in a rural county in Missouri. Their goal was to identify the interviewees' mental models of addiction recovery. Unsurprisingly, they found participants and their loved ones believed "you have to want it" to recover from addiction.

A man in his late-twenties, who quit heroin for less than three months, mentioned:

You've got to want it...it's not court ordered. It's not, I had a near-death experience, so I'm going to start shit. You have to find it in yourself that you want to change something bad enough to where you're going to stop all the BS and start living life for what it is. Be responsible for your actions (Stringfellow 2019).

Similarly, a woman in her mid-thirties, who quit methamphetamine for almost four years, stated:

I've found that unless they actually want to help themselves, there's nothing you can do to help them (Stringfellow 2019).

Drug users' loved ones felt the same way as well. In fact, a mother, with a son in recovery from heroin addiction and a daughter still actively using heroin, shared:

And when you want to help, you know how to get it. Because they're all aware of how to get the help. They've been through it already enough. And when you want the help, you'll get the help.... They just don't want to stop using. And until they're really ready, they're not going to stop using. My own children, other people's children. Until they're really ready or they're forced by locking them up, they're not gonna get help. Unless they really, really want it. You know some people get tired of being sick and tired. And when they do, they finally change. they change their whole life. They can quit using...I cut myself off until she called me and basically was ready to do something (Stringfellow 2019).

While the sentiment "you have to want it" is understandable given one's experiences, the problem with that way of thinking is it actually reinforces the addiction cycle. Dr. Stringfellow and her team concluded that insufficient evidence of "wanting it" led to loved ones withdrawing their support, triggering the need to use again.

They also discovered detaching one's support from their loved one's perceived effort in recovery—maintaining support through the highs and the lows—does little to curb drug use, but actually yields the strongest eventual recovery. Believing that recovery is based on effort is also damaging because it fails to acknowledge that addiction is a disease, and recovery doesn't happen in a straight line. Just like we saw with weight loss, addiction recovery is not solely a function of effort, and changing our mental models is a critical step in making real progress.

It's time we retire all the platitudes reinforcing how we simply need to work harder to achieve our goals. Whether you're working to overcome anxious thoughts and feelings, supporting loved ones going through addiction recovery, or navigating homelessness, one thing is clear: don't blame a lack of trying for the struggles you or others are facing; focus on reframing the thought patterns and mental models quietly yet strongly influencing your or others' potential for success.

Unlearn—S H Miller

I want to unlearn all the rules I know.
Like money in the bank equals happiness,
or getting married and having kids is a necessity in life.

I never want to watch an advertisement again
that tells me the way I am isn't okay.

I never want to be sold on what's right
because I never want to forget all the wrong.

I want to go from country to country
knowing that the people and land are a part of my own.

I want to leave this place the same way I came in.
Without guidelines or rules to tell me what's next.

REFLECTIONS

- Consider something you'd like to unlearn, like a habit or tendency. What are some daily practices you can adopt to reframe the patterns of thinking underlying that behavior?
- If you've tried to lose weight previously and didn't succeed, where did things go wrong? How can you shift your mindset to lose weight and keep it off?
- Think about an unconscious bias you have, whether it's related to race, religion, gender, age, or any other factor. Is it rooted in fact or belief? How can you become more cognizant of it and change that way of thinking?
- Why are notions of caste identity so difficult to unlearn for some Indians who moved to the United States? Are there any cultural traditions you abide by that no longer seem relevant in today's world?
- Are there any behaviors you engage in which contradict established information due to your experiences? How can you limit making exceptions and excuses based on personal experiences?

EXERCISES

- Imagine you frequently become defensive when others try to give you feedback, and your partner has recently made you intimately aware of that. Come up with three ways you can address and unlearn that tendency keeping mental models in mind:

_____

_____

- Below are a few commonly discussed topics. Pick one and see if any new insights emerge by applying a mental model lens.
    - Polarization is at an all-time high. How can we communicate and collaborate effectively with those belonging to a different political party?
    - The Great Resignation demonstrates a massive misalignment between what people are passionate about and the careers they've chosen. Where does that misalignment stem from?
    - AI is being used widely in everything from hiring decisions to distributing healthcare. Should we be concerned and why?

Superpowers

"We can change the world if we change ourselves. We just need to get hold of the old patterns of thinking and dealing with things and start listening to our inner voices and trusting our own superpowers."

—NINA HAGEN

Like most Americans, I've been obsessed with superheroes from a young age. From Superman, with his alien-like powers and near invincibility, to Batman, with his creativity and ingenuity, something about superheroes uniquely captivates us. That Marvel has launched twenty-five superhero movies in a thirteen-year window (2008–2021) is a testament to the widespread interest in the genre, not to mention the countless record-breaking box office successes (Rotten Tomatoes; Sherlock 2020).

So, it's clear: superheroes are a thing. A big thing. Even though we're all aware, outside of imaginative kids' and adults' wishful thinking, we can never be like them.

Although exposing and shifting your ingrained patterns of thinking won't give you laser eyes or super strength, doing so can unlock quasi-superpowers: the ability to learn from and influence those who disagree with you, and the clarity needed to live a more fulfilling life.

LEARNING FROM THOSE WITH WHOM WE DISAGREE

"In some ways, we will always be different. In other ways, we will always be the same. There is always room to disagree and blame, just as there is always room to take a new perspective and empathize. Understanding is a choice."

—*Vironika Tugaleva*

Why is it so hard nowadays to have conversations with people who think differently or disagree with us? And what can we do about it? It doesn't help that polarization is at an all-time high, and it certainly is challenging that social media platforms reinforce echo chambers (Gordon 2020).

Thankfully, mental models open a path forward. Something we can all do to bridge the gap between us and folks with differing viewpoints is to uncover their mental models and understand why they think that way. Doing so helps separate one's views from the individual and our feelings toward them, opening the door to more fruitful discussion. Now, the motivation for communicating shifts from proving you're right to simply understanding.

I realized there's a dire need for approaching conversations this way after seeing countless comments on divisive posts on Facebook.

It was July 16, 2019. A few days before, I had quit my first job since graduating college to figure out my life path. After taking a solo trip to South Africa, I found myself with time on my hands. I'd often end up scrolling through Facebook, being entertained by people's reactions to sensitive topics like China's treatment of Uighurs (the largest ethnic minority living in China's north-western province of Xinjiang), whether non-Black allies are doing enough to stand up for Black people, or how vegans sometimes show more care for animals than other people.

Instead of focusing on individual comments and thoughts, I analyzed the subtext (the words and meanings between the lines) to figure out whether people are capable of discussing with folks who have different perspectives. The results were mildly depressing.

As you likely guessed, nearly 99 percent of comments I read were extremely for or against the discussion topic at hand. Taking the example of Uighurs, people belonged to one of two camps: those very critical of the Chinese Communist Party (CCP) and skeptical of Uighurs fair treatment, and those very supportive of the CCP and don't see any issues with what's happening.

Virtually no one took a middle ground stance, possibly because there's an extremism bias when it comes to posting online. Nevertheless, it struck me as odd that no one even tried to understand the people on the other side of the argument or where they were coming from; instead, everyone was virtue signaling and trying to convince other people they were right, and the others were wrong.

A few comments that piqued my interest related to the treatment of Uighurs were:

Facebook User One: "[It's] also funny how so many people who know [nothing] about Chinese sociology, history, and culture just suddenly crawl out of their holes and claim to be experts on the issues. And calling others that are more informed, or of a different opinion, or *gasp,* have actually lived in Xingjian 'brainwashed' and [sponsored] by Winnie Pooh or something."

Facebook User Two: "There is no instance which justifies mass sterilization. Every person here using terrorist attacks to paint over the Uighurs and then saying Chinese people aren't like that are being hypocritical. What's happening here is genocide. There's no other way to talk about it."

Facebook User Three: "[The] comment section is gold: 1) the successful brainwashing of Han Chinese, who somehow trust info from the government that censors and lies to them and fail to recognize discrimination as they're in the dominant group, 2) the binary opposition in how people just see good or evil in the CCP when the truth is far more complex, and 3) the hypocrisy of Americans calling out these practices when we've done the same to Japanese citizens and also discriminate against minorities, albeit in more institutionalized ways."

There's a lot to unpack here on the surface. But between the lines (including the hundreds of other comments I've looked at) a clear thread emerges: people suck at understanding others' mental models, so when confronted with conflicting opinions, they get defensive or upset, judge people with whom they don't agree, and continue shouting in their respective echo chambers. Facebook User Three, which I'll admit is actually me, was a rare exception to this pattern. Only a handful of comments illustrated an appreciation for both sides of issues and hinted to the world being more gray than black and white.

You might not think this is a big deal. After all, how many people interact with and learn from people with distinct views, values, and beliefs? Unfortunately, not as many as should.

By taking the time to uncover others' mental models, you are, by definition, broadening your own perspective. It helps you learn from what's informed their mental models: their experiences, exposure to sociocultural norms, beliefs, and more. There's value in that even if you don't change their opinion on something or feel more validated in your stance.

Visit my Figma board here: **https://bit.ly/3uB8pje** *if you'd like to see the aforementioned comments and related images I created. Simply press the play button (the triangle rotated ninety degrees to the right) next to the Log In button in the top left corner and drag around each page to see everything.*

The key to having productive conversations with people you disagree with—whether your motivation is to validate your perspective, learn from theirs, or influence someone else—is to approach these virtual or physical interactions with mental models in mind.

By applying a mental model lens to these interactions, you're changing the goal of the conversation. It's no longer about proving you're right, but instead learning about the other person's way of thinking and where their mental models come from. By approaching discussions in this way, we can prevent ourselves from judging the other person for their beliefs or values and reduces the likelihood the other person gets defensive. Remember, the goal is to learn, not attack or defend.

Perhaps more importantly, it enables the other person to recognize that their mindset and perspective are shaped by their ingrained way of thinking. This is huge because the next step is for them to appreciate that their mental model is just different than yours. There is no right or wrong, just variation owing to natural differences in our exposures to media and others' mental models, beliefs informed by our experiences, and prevailing sociocultural norms.

If you can help the other person unravel why they believe the things they do, you've just created a golden opportunity to influence them and possibly change their mindset. Take the conflict I frequently experience with my parents around my life choices as an example.

As first-generation immigrants, they came to California in the 1980s from humble beginnings in Hyderabad, a large state in south India. As if moving to a different country wasn't difficult enough, they had to adapt the cultural attitudes and platitudes, life lessons, and beliefs they internalized as truths growing up in Indian villages. Naturally, some of the changes were easier to adapt than others.

My parents, like most Indians at the time, had an arranged marriage. My mom was just sixteen years old, and my parents had only met each other a handful of times before their families orchestrated their marriage. When I share with my parents my reluctance to get married at the age of twenty-seven, which would be considered primetime for men based on their generational values and upbringing, I'm thankful they don't push back. Both are supportive of me focusing on my life before taking that big next step.

I'm eternally grateful their pattern of thinking related to marriage has changed. But despite only being a generation apart, at times it feels like it might as well be centuries. Part of where that feeling comes from is knowing, to them, the idea of arranged marriage and marrying young is familiar and agreeable. Even though those things would drive me absolutely crazy. It's because their mindset and perspective on topics like marriage are rooted in traditional values they grew up with and their own lived experiences. It took years of exposure to a completely different perspective on marriage—love-based and happening much later in life—through movies, TV, and American friends to shift their way of thinking.

But when I share with them that I don't know if I want kids, things get difficult. "So, you don't want us to have grandkids? How could you say that, when our purpose in life is to have offspring and take care of them? Who will take care of you when you get old?" These are just a few of the frustrating comments I regularly deal with.

I hope one day my parents understand where I'm coming from. Until then, I'm endeavoring to understand where they're coming from and why they feel that way; perhaps it's due to the influence of the sociocultural attitudes they were exposed to, or maybe it's because of the religious messages they've internalized espousing the importance of having kids.

Whatever the reasons, I've found that understanding and respecting where they're coming from and why without judgment has been incredibly helpful. By starting conversations off on that foot, we avoid common pitfalls making people defensive, like feeling you're not being understood or feeling attacked for what you think. Over time, and after many months of discussion, I've noticed my parents are slowly understanding my perspective because I've been approaching our conversations with their mental models in mind. They're beginning to appreciate why my way of thinking differs from theirs, instead of reacting negatively to it.

Time will tell whether they'll ever be okay with my desire to be child-free, but the path forward looks a lot clearer now that I've taken that crucial first step. Being more patient with one another, learning from others, and changing others' mindsets are just a few of many benefits that come from an appreciation of our and others' mental models. Doing so on a broader level can have profound implications for individuals and our society as a whole.

You might be wondering, "This all sounds great, but how do I actually go about doing this?" That's completely fair. To be honest, it won't happen overnight. But the key to exercising this capability—focusing on understanding others' mental models instead of taking what they say personally—is to continuously expose yourself to people who disagree with you and have different values.

Sometimes, that's not always feasible. Imagine for a moment you identify as a progressive in San Francisco (I'm an Independent, by the way) looking to broaden your perspective and challenge your mental models by speaking with people on the conservative end of the political spectrum. Unfortunately, given how politically homogeneous the Bay Area is, that'll happen when pigs fly. No amount of using Bumble BFF (a way to meet new friends in your area), attending Meetups, or participating in similar activities will realistically change that.

Thankfully, the internet has made it easy to get exposed to groups of like-minded people, for better or worse. Something to consider is visiting news sites of the opposing political party, in this case Fox News, to observe the mental models of the people consuming its content and engaging with it through comments. Yes, this may overexpose you to intense ways of thinking due to extremism bias with posting online, but it gets the job done.

Over time, if you pay attention to the patterns between the lines instead of focusing on what people are saying, you'll realize Fox News fans have really different mental models than you. You can see part of why that's the case: they're surrounded by people (virtually and sometimes physically, as well) who share their mental model and constantly validate it. You'll probably notice that for some people, the religious values they grew up with and the moral codes they inherited really shape their perspective, on everything from abortion to LGBTQ+ rights.

The more you slowly become more aware of others' mental models, the more you'll realize that perhaps there are truths hidden in them and others' lived experiences. Like how people who oppose abortion and gay marriage on religious grounds cling to religion because it gives them a sense of purpose, community, and clarity to approach the chaos of life.

Or, for the people who oppose massive government spending out of concerns for growing biopower (the administration and regulation of human life at the level of the population and the individual body) and rising inflation, the necessity of being cautious of large, controlling governments and overspending. One's religious upbringing and ideological exposure strongly shape one's mental models, which is both beautiful and extremely powerful. More importantly, those beliefs don't make them bad people. They just have different mental models than you do.

Growing up in the Bay Area with Liberal parents, it's no surprise I felt more aligned with the political Left for much of my life. But after consuming more conservative-leaning content for the better part of a year, coupled with having more conversations with folks on the conservative end of the political spectrum, my political beliefs have shifted toward the middle. I no longer believe in a black and white dichotomy between Liberals and Republicans, or that one side is "right." Rather, I've come to appreciate the truths in each party's ideas as well as the lies.

By continuing to expose yourself to people, phenomena, and life priorities breaking your existing ways of thinking, you'll find it easier and easier to speak with contrarian thinkers. Who knows, you might actually learn a thing or two.

LIVING A FULFILLING LIFE

"Authenticity is the daily practice of letting go who we think we're supposed to be and embracing who we are."
—Brené Brown

How much of your life is based on others' expectations of you? Or, put another way, what aspects of your life have been influenced by your mental models? I ask myself these questions ever more frequently, and I'm increasingly frustrated by the answers I've come up with.

But regularly questioning the "what" behind the "why"—the ingrained patterns of thinking shaping my conscious thoughts and actions—has helped me break free. It can help you to live a more fulfilling life as well, professionally and personally.

In the US, there's a pervasive, sticky mental model influencing us to believe a good and successful life is characterized by our wealth, and we should work to make money until we retire. Only then should we begin to follow our passions.

Excuse me, but...why? Why wouldn't we do what we're passionate about when we're young and have energy? And why does making the most money possible matter more than our actual happiness and fulfillment—aside from maintaining our needs and securing our status within the system of capitalism?

If you pause to challenge the ingrained ways of thinking about our career paths, work-life balance, and the meaning of work in general, perhaps you'll realize your ingrained ways of thinking are nudging you toward a life you don't really want; they're hurting you, not serving you.

But if you fail to introspect on these invisible filters, you might find yourself in a difficult situation. Like my friend John (not his real name) and his ongoing struggle to pursue happiness. John was surrounded in college by a community of like-minded folks who held the finance—which they pretentiously pronounced *fin-ants*—industry in the highest regard. Naturally, when it came time to think about his full-time job, John gravitated toward the same well-trodden path many in his fraternity walked before him. He joined a top investment bank in the Bay Area after graduating and continued climbing the gilded ladder from investment banking to private equity, having most recently landed in venture capital.

John's career trajectory, on paper, seems like a deliberate, well-thought-out plan by someone who knows what he wants and charges toward it.

Nope. He has no clue what he really enjoys, never making the space or time to figure that out. What keeps him sane are the fruits of his excel labor and the fun he has through it: luxury travel, fine dining, and seeing his large, growing bank account.

But he literally and figuratively has gotten lost in the sauce. Nevertheless, he's somewhat aware that he doesn't find his job fulfilling and knows he must make a change one day or another. That day just never seems to come.

Despite John's frustration with his career choices, he hasn't taken the time to understand the "what" behind his "why." If he did, he'd realize he's on this path not out of his own volition. Rather, he's put himself in this position because he enjoys the perks, finds it easier not to think about what actually fulfills him, and is strongly influenced by the deeply held beliefs of the people he surrounds himself with.

How likely is it that we'll take the time to expose and question our mental models once they become so deeply rooted? Once we're caught in the proverbial rat race, it's difficult to imagine life moving at a different pace. We can't hope to change our life trajectory unless we first challenge the mental models filtering our perspectives and mindsets. Just like a company in dire need of innovating to survive, we can't rely on the mindsets that have gotten us to where we are. No, we need to transform them and ourselves.

We also can't depend on another unprecedented event like a global pandemic to trigger thinking pattern changes, like it did for the 15.5 million Americans who quit their job in "The Great Resignation" (Dean 2021). Anthony Klotz, an organizational psychologist and professor at Texas A&M University, coined the phrase and shared: "It's not just about getting another job, or leaving the workforce, it's about taking control of your work and personal life, and making a big decision—resigning—to accomplish that" (Smith 2022). As of this writing, the latest figures showed 4.5 million people voluntarily left their positions in November: that's 3 percent of the non-farm workforce (Zagorsky 2022).

Maybe "The Great Resignation" happened because people had more time to focus on their hobbies working from home, or people realized—after seeing so many people pass away due to COVID—that life is short. Whatever the case may be, while these new leases on life are commendable, how long will this shock to our systems persist? Instead of hoping our mindsets continue changing due to external forces, we should focus on being mindful of and re-evaluating our mental models.

Frequently questioning whether they align with our feelings, values, and goals is key because what you discover might surprise you. It may be time for a new filter: a fresh mindset, perspective, and way of understanding the world and your place in it.

Questioning your mental models doesn't just help you find more fulfillment in your professional life but in your personal life as well. It can help us notice and address insidious patterns of thinking enabling unhealthy behaviors like our coping mechanisms. And once we've done that, we can leverage healthy patterns of thinking to pick up and stick with new, fulfilling habits and hobbies.

For the unfamiliar, coping mechanisms are the strategies people use in the face of stress, trauma, or even boredom to help manage painful or difficult emotions. Although they can help people adjust to stressful events and maintain their emotional well-being, they aren't always healthy or desirable. A few unhealthy coping mechanisms we may all relate to include isolating ourselves, overeating, buying expensive things we don't need, and using drugs.

Sadly, many have turned to unhealthy coping mechanisms in the face of COVID-19. A CDC survey found that, during the pandemic, 13.3 percent of adults reported struggling with new or increased substance use (Beek 2021). Dr. Marilyn Sibery, who specializes in substance use disorder and works with dozens of patients in her Westchester private practice, has noticed a significant increase in drug and alcohol abuse within her field.

I'm seeing people who have alcohol use disorders who maybe were managing before COVID-19, and now they're just drinking a lot more. Substances are used as a way to cope. It's not an effective overall coping mechanism, but definitely in the beginning, it might feel like it is. And it might help ease that anxiety or depression or loneliness, but it usually starts to take on a life of its own (Beek 2021).

Reece and his partner recounted to BBC's Mona McAlinden that they experienced this for themselves. Like most of us at the beginning of lockdown, they made big plans to fill their extra time, which was substantial because, as hairdressers, the couple went from working full-time to being at home. All day. Every day.

They came up with elaborate plans to pass the time, like deciding to paint their deck and house and upholster their furniture. But just ten weeks later, Reece reported "we've given up doing that" to the hosts of BBC Scotland's *Unlocked* podcast (McAlinden 2020).

As the empty days passed, the weight of their free time became too heavy to lift; boredom soon started creeping in. That coupled with stress from isolation and unemployment led to some unfortunate lifestyle changes. Reece shared:

> *Before lockdown, we'd have a couple of joints around the weekend. After lockdown, it was becoming every day. We used to wait until about eight o'clock at night. But then it got to one o'clock, three o'clock in the afternoon and we thought, should we be smoking it this early? But then we thought there's nothing else to do, we're stuck in the house, so why not (McAlinden 2020)?*

I can intimately relate to Reece and his partner's experiences. Early on in the lockdown, I'd smoke weed and eat unhealthy food every now and then to help with my anxiety and boredom. At that point, it was like adding a little garam masala to my life. But over the course of a few weeks, my periodic smoking became a nearly daily habit, and I noticed

I'd gained at least ten pounds from a lack of exercise and munchie-induced unhealthy eating.

Turns out my life needed a lot of spice, and what started out as temporary relief slowly morphed into the only vehicles through which I could unwind and relax, which was sad, and I knew it. But what I wasn't aware of, until later, were the destructive patterns of thinking enabling these behaviors by minimizing or disregarding the consequences of my actions.

"But smoking weed often isn't that bad for me. What's the worst that can happen, I get the munchies?"

"I don't do it all the time, just every now and then."

"It's temporary, just something to get me through the pandemic. I'll stop smoking so often in a few months, so there's no need to worry."

While these thoughts seem harmless on their own, taken together they reveal a destructive pattern of thinking which dismisses and minimizes the severity of the issues at hand. Only after reaching a breaking point—realizing my clothes weren't fitting and being unable to get high because of my high weed tolerance—did I begin questioning the subtle thinking patterns leading me down this dark path.

It took months, but I slowly realized I shouldn't need drugs or food to cope with the frustration, anxiety, and boredom I was feeling, and the stories I unknowingly told myself were getting in the way. When I felt bored or wanted to unwind, I trained myself to opt for things I enjoyed instead of things that made me feel chemically fuzzy. For example, I'd write haiku, play the trumpet, or take a walk; two of which were new hobbies I wouldn't have picked up otherwise.

My mental models reassured me that my excessive weed use was fine, and the decision-making was legitimate, but by recognizing these destructive mental models and making different choices, I initiated satisfying, healthy change into my life.

So how do we hold a mirror up to ourselves to identify destructive mental models before they wreak havoc on our lives? One strategy to help expose your mental models is intentionally dissociating. I know that sounds strange (and runs contrary to every true crime show you've ever seen), but bear with me for a moment.

Dictionary.com defines dissociation as: to sever the association of (oneself); separate: to withdraw from association.

You've probably heard of this word before in the context of psychological conditions, like schizophrenia or borderline personality disorder. Why would anyone want to intentionally dissociate? Let's put it in the context of dealing with anxiety. Consider thinking of dissociating not in the clinical sense—as our brain trying to protect us from a traumatic experience—but rather an intentional way of detaching from our first-person emotional feelings of anxiety.

Examining one's pattern of anxiety from a distance can highlight how certain situations can trigger anxious feelings, and we can control how we react and respond to those situations and fears about what may happen in the future. By seeing ourselves from a third-person point of view, or at a distance, we can look at our mental models objectively and choose an alternative thought or belief that helps us overcome anxiety and other challenges.

It's worth considering activities that can shine a light on your thought patterns and behaviors, like journaling and introspection.

Journaling daily is a great way to express one's thoughts, and there's a certain catharsis in that. But the secret to finding our mental models and walking toward fulfillment is to *read between our own lines*, looking for patterns in our thoughts instead of focusing on the content itself, like how I analyzed Facebook comments. In other words, after you submit a journal entry, the next step is to look for ingrained patterns of thinking influencing how you're feeling, thinking, or reacting to situations.

While journaling can be an effective tool to identify mental models if done properly, introspection is a tricky activity because it often yields no or negative results.

Introspection is arguably the most universally hailed path to internal self-awareness. After all, what better way is there to increase our self-knowledge than to look inward, to delve deeply into our experiences and emotions, and to understand why we are the way we are? When we reflect, we might be trying to understand our feelings ("Why am I so upset after that meeting?"), questioning our beliefs ("Do I really believe what I think I believe?"), or figuring out our future ("Why am I unhappy at work?").

I don't know about you, but I often find myself spending an endless amount of time in self-reflection only to emerge with no more self-insight than when I started. And I'm not alone. A study of more than 14,000 university students showed introspection was associated with poorer well-being (Park 2012). Other research suggests self-analyzers tend to have more anxiety, fewer positive social experiences, and more negative attitudes about themselves (Nezlek 2002; Stein 2014).

In truth, introspection can cloud our self-perceptions and unleash a host of unintended consequences. Sometimes, it may surface unproductive and upsetting emotions that can swamp us and impede positive action.

Tasha Eurich, a *New York Times* best-selling author and a PhD in organizational psychology, wanted to unravel why that happens. She and her team compiled a group of fifty *self-awareness unicorns:* people rated high in self-awareness (both by themselves and by others) but who had started out with only low to moderate self-awareness (Eurich 2017).

When they analyzed the unicorns' speech patterns, what stood out is they universally reported asking *what* often and *why* rarely. In interview transcripts, the word *why* appeared fewer than 150 times, while the word *what* appeared more than 1,000 times. One self-awareness unicorn, a forty-two-year-old mother who walked away from a career as a lawyer when she finally realized there was no joy for her in that path, explained it this way:

> *If you ask why, [I think] you're putting yourself into a victim mentality.... When I feel anything other than peace,*

I say "What's going on?" or "What am I feeling?" or "What is the dialogue inside my head?" or "What's another way to see this situation?" or "What can I do to respond better?" (Eurich 2017)

At times, asking *what* instead of *why* can force us to name our emotions, thought patterns, and tendencies. Imagine you're in a terrible mood after work one day. Asking "Why do I feel so down?" might elicit unhelpful answers like "Because I hate Mondays!" or "Because I'm just a negative person!"

Instead, if you ask, "What things are influencing me to be negative?" you could realize your ingrained way of thinking leads to stress triggers—like feeling overwhelmed at work, hunger, and exhaustion—to push you into a negative spiral. Armed with that knowledge and before you spiral downward, you might decide to fix yourself dinner, call a friend, or watch your favorite TV show.

Identifying mental models through introspection requires asking difficult *what* questions but can be surprisingly effective. My decision to leave a promising career in venture capital to pursue opportunities in the climate tech sector and focus on writing was the result of asking myself these kinds of questions. I ultimately realized that no amount of money or prestige would ever truly fulfill me, and I'm at my best when I'm creating or building. While my future is a lot less certain than before, I'm happier than I've ever been and excited to figure out my own path. I'm willing to bet you will be too if you so choose.

The key to living a fulfilling life is to continuously hold a mirror up to ourselves and expose destructive patterns of thinking limiting us personally and professionally. Identifying and shifting those mental models enables us to achieve incredible things, like pursuing our passions and trading in unhealthy coping mechanisms for hobbies and attitudes that spark joy.

How can we possibly change these sticky, ingrained ways of thinking?

A Superhero–Naomi Woodcock

A superhero brings about justice
so that humankind can have peace

A superhero is always kind
especially when helping the blind

A superhero has great wisdom
and uses it to protect their kingdom

A superhero has to be brave
so they can help the trapped escape

A superhero can act as a shield
they protect us and never yield

A superhero has to be generous
they give up their time and strength for us

But a superhero might not be like you think
they can be everyday people so you might not make the link

An everyday hero might not be able to fly
maybe sometimes they're also a little shy

But an everyday hero can make a difference
because they are prepared to go the distance.

REFLECTIONS

- Below are just a few superpowers we can gain by applying mental models to our lives. Do any other superpowers come to mind for you?
  - Influencing others
  - Learning from others
  - Pursuing what fulfills us
  - Making choices avoiding pressure to do/be/act a certain way
  - Mitigating anxious tendencies
  - Solving problems more effectively
  - Adopting a positive mindset
  - Combating coping mechanisms
  - Enabling habit change
- If you're working, are you happy in your career choice? Does it fulfill you? If not, why didn't you try something else or take bigger risks? What stops you from taking that risk now?
- When you feel bored, anxious, or stressed, what coping mechanisms do you turn to? If they aren't healthy habits, what are some you'd like to replace them with? How can you avoid letting triggers—which are unavoidable—drive you to your coping mechanisms?

EXERCISES

- Find someone online or in person that disagrees with you about something important—think politics, ways of seeing the world, religion, etc.—and communicate with them. Anything from responding to strangers' posts on

Reddit to speaking with your Uber driver counts. Try to avoid associating that individual's beliefs with their character and endeavor to understand why they think the way they do. Was the conversation more fruitful? What did you learn about them, yourself, or the world?

- Pick something that's made you feel down or sad recently. For example, I've felt lonely throughout COVID-19 as close friends have moved elsewhere. Now, spend ten minutes to reflect on what is actually causing that unhappiness and what you can do about it. When I engaged in that exercise, for instance, I realized my loneliness stemmed from an ingrained belief that we must have a core social group or community to be happy. Upon further reflection, I began to see how that notion prevented me from finding new friends I connect with on deeper levels and how having a primary social group may not be such a good thing after all. What did you realize or uncover from your introspection?

Alter, Don't Falter

"Victories over ingrained patterns of thought are not won in a day or a year."

—ISAAC ASIMOV

There once was a ten-year-old boy who decided to study Judo, despite losing his left arm in a car accident. After a long search, the boy started taking lessons with an old Japanese Judo master. He performed well, but he couldn't understand why his master only taught him one move even after three months of training. "Sensei," the boy finally said, "Shouldn't I be learning more moves?" (Lenehan 1994).

"This is the only move you know, but this is the only move you'll ever need to know," the sensei replied (Lenehan 1994). Not quite understanding, but believing in his teacher, the boy kept training.

Several months later, the sensei took the boy to his first tournament. Surprising himself, the boy easily won his first two matches. The third match proved to be more difficult, but after some time, his opponent became impatient and charged; the boy deftly used his one move to win the match. Still amazed by his success, the boy was now in the finals.

This time, his opponent was bigger, stronger, and more experienced. Like a scene out of the Bible, he was a disabled David, facing Goliath. And for a while, the boy appeared outmatched. Concerned the one-armed boy might get hurt, the referee called a timeout.

He was about to stop the match when the boy's sensei intervened. "No," the sensei insisted, "Let him continue." Soon after the match resumed, the boy's opponent made a critical mistake: he dropped his guard. Instantly, the boy used his one move to pin him. With that, the boy had won the match and the tournament—he was the champion. On their way home, the boy and his sensei reviewed every move in each match (Lenehan 1994).

Suddenly, the boy summoned the courage to ask what was really on his mind. "Sensei, how did I win the tournament with only one move?"

"You won for two reasons," the Sensei answered. "First, you've almost mastered one of the most difficult throws in all of Judo. And second, the only known defense for that move is for your opponent to grab your left arm" (Lenehan 1994).

Sometimes, what we perceive to be weaknesses can become our greatest strengths. All it takes is adapting to the situation and focusing on what we have control over. And that rings true for mental models as well: left alone, they can cause invisible and observable damage, but they can become our greatest assets with the proper care. Knowing we can never get rid of them, nor should we try to given how useful they can be, we must focus on changing them to align with our values and achieve our goals. In this chapter, we'll examine several tools and techniques helping us expose and shift our ingrained patterns of thinking, including psychedelic-assisted therapy, meditation, and cognitive behavioral therapy.

PSYCHING UP TO PSYCHEDELICS

"Psychedelics are illegal not because a loving government is concerned that you may jump out of a third story window. Psychedelics are illegal because they dissolve opinion structures and culturally laid down models of behavior and information processing. They open you up to the possibility that everything you know is wrong."

—*Terence McKenna*

And just like that, we stumbled into a verdant clearing tucked away in Berkeley's Fire Trails. A preliminary scan revealed we were alone safe from others' judgment and wonder. No more than a minute passed, and we dropped to the ground as if compelled by gravity. I remember it was moist, soft like a feather, and alive, beating with the movement of hundreds of insects. I couldn't get up.

Nor did I want to, really. What felt like several hours flew by (it was probably closer to thirty minutes), and in that time, we forgot about everything: ongoing existential crises, the mundanities of everyday life, and our identities as individuals.

No, I wasn't drunk or high. I was tripping on psychedelics.

A few hours prior, I spontaneously took a large dose of psilocybin (a natural psychedelic colloquially known as "magic mushrooms") with a close friend. It was near the end of the spring semester of our sophomore year, and in classic college fashion, we quite frankly had nothing better to do. In hindsight I should've done far more research, but nevertheless I was intrigued to experience a substance so powerful that the government banned scientists from studying it in the sixties and seventies.

To be fair, the demise of psychedelic drug research wasn't solely due to the "War on Drugs" campaign and the potency of psychedelic substances. But it was hastened by tighter regulation of pharmaceutical research, the failure of controlled trials to live up to the claims of psychedelic advocates, and the pharmaceutical industry's lack of interest in funding clinical trials (Hall 2021).

In the weeks leading up to this "trip" (a term which broadly refers to any psychedelic experience), I was already in a spiritual mood. After months of nonstop debauchery, I vowed to take a break from drinking and began meditating daily. Around the same time, I started reading more about the inhumane treatment of animals by the meat industry and started to question my food choices. Maybe that's why my first trip ever took on a more spiritual bent, or maybe it was just meant to be.

After ingesting a handful of psilocybin mushrooms, which look and taste like something rotten that you'd normally throw away, we waited half an hour for the nausea to subside. A bit dazed but eager, we traipsed through northern Berkeley to reach the Fire Trails. Named because they were intended to stop the spread of flames, the Fire Trails are in the lush hills above the main campus. Just a few minutes away from town, they offer a beautiful escape into majestic oak forests, towering redwoods, and glimmering grasslands.

Less than two hours into our journey, slowed by small strides and deep conversation, my friend and I stumbled upon a grassy clearing surrounded by gorgeous oak trees. We'd been walking for miles, and without saying a word, we each took a moment to feel the earth beneath us.

I was quickly overwhelmed by a profound sense of oneness with the earth and all living things. That feeling only intensified as we kept exploring the area; reaching its zenith after a chance encounter with a doe just a few feet away. Maybe it's because I'm a diehard fan of *Princess Mononoke*, one of auteur Hayao Miyazaki's masterpieces featuring an incredible scene with a deer as the spirit of the forest, but I felt like Mother Nature was trying to tell me something. A few hours later, the trip reached a pleasant conclusion, but that feeling of oneness stuck with me.

While I didn't know it at the time, my casual encounter with psychedelics would change me in profound ways. Perhaps the most radical transformation was perceiving life with a completely new outlook: not seeing the world as a combination of billions of separate life forms, but as one interconnected web. Admittedly, I didn't soberly feel the same, heightened sense of unity that I had experienced on psilocybin, but once the door had been opened, it couldn't be shut.

A few days passed before I decided to become vegetarian. I quit meat cold turkey—pun intended! After all, if all living things are connected, we must respect and support one another. My blind participation in the system of animal agriculture was doing the exact opposite.

Although my other psychedelic experiences haven't been as eye-opening, by shifting my state of consciousness, they've enabled me to perceive myself, the world, and my role in it in new ways. But to be clear, this isn't an endorsement for recreational psychedelic drug use. I *do not* advocate taking psychedelics on your own at home or with friends. Just like how you wouldn't try to vaccinate yourself, it's critical to take psychedelics in controlled, safe settings. Looking back, I'm honestly shocked I've never had a bad trip—who knows what could've gone wrong?

But without a doubt, my psychedelic experiences have been an incredibly helpful tool in my battle to challenge my ingrained ways of thinking. And others feel the same way.

Keith Abraham never expected to find himself deep in the Peruvian jungle, drinking a powerful hallucinogenic brew from a dirty Coca-Cola bottle. A former member of the elite British Parachute Regiment, he enlisted in the US military after 9/11 to "hunt down the bad guys" (Perry 2021). After a relatively uneventful tour of Iraq, in 2008, he was sent to fight in Afghanistan's Helmand Province, one of the world's deadliest battlegrounds. Early on, his unit was ambushed. And in the first burst of gunfire, he saw two close friends die. Like so many other soldiers, Keith eventually returned home wracked with a debilitating cocktail of grief, depression, and post-traumatic stress disorder.

He hoped returning to civilian life would offer some relief. He was off to a great start; he quickly landed a new, high-flying job at JP Morgan, but he knew he was falling apart. He'd sit in his office with sweat pouring from his hands and face. His hair fell out in his sleep. He could never escape the feeling that his body was being held in a stress position.

Conventional antidepressants just made him feel worse, so when a friend suggested he travel to South America to try ayahuasca—a traditional plant medicine containing the hallucinogen DMT—he figured he had nothing to lose. In April of 2014, he flew to Lima and returned a changed man. "Psychologically, I knew that I'd been healed," he says (Perry 2021).

Psychedelic drugs act on receptors for serotonin, a neurotransmitter affecting mood, appetite, sleep regulation, and other high-level brain functions. Emerging evidence suggests psychedelics enhance the brain's neuroplasticity, which helps users escape from rigid patterns of thought (de Vos 2021). Subtler effects include increased insight into one's own habitual patterns of thinking, behavior, personal problems, and past experiences. The receptive state the drugs confer opens the door to fresh ideas, just like how my psilocybin experience helped me feel and realize that life is interconnected. On death's door, others report using psilocybin greatly reduced the anxiety and depression they felt about their impending deaths (Slater 2012). Some have even broken cycles of addiction, like smoking for months on end, due to their powerful psychedelic experiences (O'Neill 2019).

Keith's experience healing from the traumas of war and stories like his are why Army Ranger-turned-psychedelic advocate Jesse Gould started the Heroic Hearts Project. You see, Jesse's story is similar to Keith's in many ways. Like Keith, Jesse was deployed to Afghanistan on three tours and pushed to his limits physically, mentally, and spiritually each time. By the time his duty position ended, the war was winding down, and he was ready for the next chapter of his life. Jesse also found himself in a high-flying job in finance at an international company, but the situation spiraled downhill quickly as his mental health deteriorated. Jesse admitted:

On reflection, it's clear that even during my time in the military there were mental health issues always arising. And given the lifestyle or distractions of the situation I was able to ignore it or justify that it was okay. So, if you're a Ranger or any special ops, it's a "work hard, play hard" mentality and things are so fast-paced you don't really have time to actually realize you might be affected by your experience. When I got to that corporate job, when things slowed down to civilian life, I realized the way I was living was unhealthy. My issues manifested in severe anxiety to the point where I had to miss work due to panic attacks that lasted a day or several days, severe depression or this grayness of the world, and self-medicating with alcohol to numb the anxiety and pain.

Thankfully, Jesse saw these red flags. He became alarmed that "more and more days were unhappy or bland," and he knew it was no way to live. He sought help at the VA, but it wasn't helpful, and he saw how limited mental health treatment options were outside of a regimen of prescription medicines with severe side effects. When he heard about ayahuasca, a psychoactive plant used as spiritual medicine among the indigenous peoples of the Amazon basin, he was intrigued despite never having an interest in psychedelics. He left his job, packed up his things and took a plane to Peru.

I went there and found a week-long retreat. Going through the ceremonies was really challenging, taxing, and frightening, but the end of it brought a lot of insight and healing. It helped change me physically, psychologically, and spiritually. It pushed me to the edge where I confronted my fears feeling everything, but eventually through the process, it taught me how to get to this tranquil state away from the anxiety and depression. The whole week was going back and forth in those states until I allowed and accepted that I could be in this tranquil spot. So, it almost was training me and this muscle I can use to sidestep anxiety. I still feel those things today, of course, but they're no longer debilitating.

Jesse's profound experience opened the door to patterns of thinking and feeling that he was struggling to access and continues to help him sidestep his mental health challenges. It's important to note that a psychedelic experience in and of itself won't shift your mental models long-term, but they can be a critical step in the journey.

Seeing the spectacular changes in himself and those around him made Jesse rethink the things he's been told about psychedelics, and it inspired him to help other veterans in his network struggling with suicide and depression. In 2017, Jesse launched a 501(c)(3) non-profit, the Heroic Hearts Project, to help veterans heal from PTSD, trauma, anxiety, and depression by helping finance and connect them with vetted psychedelic therapies. Organizations like the Heroic Hearts Project, coupled with advances in research, are shifting our shared mental model around drug use and helping people embrace the virtues and values of psychedelics.

Used in conjunction with therapy, research has shown psychedelics can help treat historically difficult-to-treat conditions by essentially "reshaping" the way "parts of the brain talk to each other," says Jennifer Mitchell, a neuroscientist and professor in the departments of neurology, psychiatry, and behavioral sciences at the University of California San Francisco (Stieg 2021). With psilocybin, for instance, it is believed the "drug boosts connectivity in the brain and increases neuroplastic states," which are the brain's ability to reorganize and adapt, says Dr. Stephen Ross, associate professor of psychiatry at the NYU Grossman School of Medicine, who has been conducting clinical trials on psilocybin-assisted therapy for the past sixteen years (Stieg 2021).

While psychedelic research in the US is in its infancy due to prevailing stigmas, Europe seems to be undergoing a psychedelic science renaissance. In fact, about a third of all experimental studies with psilocybin—including how it can treat alcohol use disorder and depression—are happening in Europe (Tatala 2020). Still, the future of psychedelic-assisted therapies in the US seems bright. Novel models like Rainfall Medicine, where patients are administered small doses of ketamine in a clinical setting supervised by doctors and therapists to treat mood disorders, PTSD, or addiction, appear to be where the industry is heading.

Startups like Field Trip, which offers ketamine-driven psychedelic exploration sessions, are so confident in the promise of these drugs that it's building seventy-five centers for psychedelic therapy over the next three years. But further clinical use and mainstream adoption depends on people's ability to pay for treatments with insurance, which won't change until psychedelics are no longer federally classified as Schedule I drugs.

Science has only brushed the surface of psychedelics' therapeutic possibilities, but the early results are promising. Psychedelic-assisted therapies administered in safe, clinical settings are worth considering to alter our states of mind and mental models as well.

MASTERING OUR MINDS WITH MEDITATION

"Meditation is not about stopping thoughts, but recognizing that we are more than our thoughts and our feelings."
—*Arianna Huffington (Pajer 2021)*

Meditation can treat severe depression. I know that sounds like a tall claim, but Keri Wiginton's story might convince you otherwise.

Keri can't recall the moment when her depression set in but admits she's "been on the wrong side of happy since [she] was four, when [her] parents split" (Wiginton 2018). Perhaps there was nothing she could do about it given her father's history of mental illness and how adverse childhood events increase the risk. Her first diagnosis didn't come until her final year of high school. After six months of "spontaneous crying spells, bouts of paranoia, and a diagnosis of irritable bowel syndrome, I told my mom I needed help," Keri shared (Wiginton 2018). Eventually, a psychiatrist diagnosed Keri with clinical depression at seventeen and suggested Prozac, but she was hesitant to try it.

She managed to get by without medication in college. Even though there were a few spells of gloom, they only lasted a few days at a time. But that changed soon enough. Anxiety started plaguing her once she started her career as a newspaper photo-journalist, and her depression settled in "like a virus that wouldn't go away" (Wiginton 2018). Keri recounts feeling like she was going through the motions and "trudging through every day with lead-filled boots and a rock on her chest" (Wiginton 2018).

She tried all sorts of things to get better. Positive lifestyle changes didn't make much of a difference. Nor did talk therapy. No amount of socializing or exercising made getting out of bed any easier. These futile attempts led her to all sorts of medication—SSRIs (selective serotonin reuptake inhibitors) for anxiety and SNRIs for depression—but they failed to relieve her mental health challenges and had nasty side effects. The weight gain and constipation were unbearable for a few weeks, let alone a lifetime. Without many real options left, Keri turned to meditation in a last-ditch effort.

Nowadays, it's pervasive in American culture, but let's take a step back to unpack what meditation refers to. "Meditation refers to a set of cognitive training techniques and practices that aim to monitor and regulate attention, perception, emotion, and homeostasis (e.g., breathing rate)" (Millière 2018). Similar techniques and practices have been developed in many different cultures and spiritual traditions, resulting in over 100 varieties of meditation. Most scientific research on the topic has focused on techniques originating in the Buddhist tradition from China, Tibet, India, and Southeast Asia. Nonetheless, there are a growing number of studies on meditative practices from other contemplative traditions including yogic, Hindu, Christian, Sufi, shamanic, and transcendental practices.

Coming back to Keri, she decided to try meditation when pharmaceuticals let her down, sharing:

A growing body of research supported the use of mindfulness techniques for preventing a depression relapse, and a friend of mine who battled anxiety had found relief through the practice. I downloaded the Headspace app on my phone and set aside time to try it out. My mind felt jumbled for the first few ten-minute sessions with Andy Puddicombe, the former Buddhist monk who guides listeners step by step through meditation. But after about a week, I noticed a shift in my thinking. In the session, Puddicombe told me not to stop my negative thoughts, but to pause and notice them, then return my focus to my breathing. This helped me distance myself from the ideas running around in my head (Wiginton 2018).

Keri stuck with her meditation session daily, and after a month reported she saw her thought patterns, or mental models, more clearly. She noted, "I was struck by how often I was caught up in a negative thought loop: was I doing well at work? Did I get new wrinkles? Is the economy going to crash? The more I observed this habit, the more I interrupted it before it spiraled out of control. I could see the worry, and I could let it go without dwelling on it" (Wiginton, 2018).

Meditation is such an incredible self-help tool because it provides a unique sense of clarity into our thought patterns. As Jon Kabat-Zinn, author of *Wherever You Go, There You Are*, puts it, "Meditation does not involve trying to change your thinking by thinking some more. It involves watching thought itself. The watching is the holding. By watching your thoughts without being drawn into them, you can learn something profoundly liberating about thinking itself, which may help you to be less of a prisoner of those thought patterns."

Keri's story illustrates how meditation can shine a light on disruptive or undesirable patterns of thinking. While there are many forms of meditation worth trying, one I'd strongly recommend is transcendental meditation, commonly referred to as TM.

Mark Lubeck, an old colleague and a talented UX designer, has spent most of his life practicing and teaching others TM. Unlike other forms of meditation, TM involves silently repeating a mantra for fifteen to twenty minutes a day, typically while sitting with your eyes closed. It's one of the most widely practiced meditation techniques, learned by over ten million people (Transcendental Meditation 2019).

If you've tried any form of meditation before, you know that it's a notoriously difficult practice to stick with, despite a plethora of apps and tools like Calm, Headspace, and others. Part of the challenge is the ingrained perception that meditation is a difficult thing to do, limiting adoption and consistent adherence.

Mark recalls how he has given hundreds of lectures in public and private about meditation and the mental models he frequently encountered:

> *Typically, the mental model of meditation prevalent for my career is that meditation is a hard thing to do, requiring concentration and discipline. So, people are reluctant to meditate and question their own ability to do it. "My mind is so busy; how can I meditate?" What's interesting about that to a teacher of TM is that we argue it's untrue. People's mental model of their own mind is that "I'm fluttered with thoughts and there's no logic or reason behind this. And if I don't understand it, how could I control it?" Some traditions describe the mind as a "drunken monkey stung by a bee." The ideal state is supposed to be subtle, peaceful, and blissful, and to overcome the activity of the mind requires self-control. It turns out the mind doesn't jump around without purpose.*

The TM technique is a way of taking thought as a vehicle and using the natural tendency of attention to help the mind settle down on its own thought process and experience self-awareness. Like other forms of meditation, TM helps us uncover and address our mental models by equipping us with the ability to observe our thought patterns almost like a third-party viewer. Instead of reacting to our thoughts or spiraling because of them, meditation teaches us to simply notice them and let them go.

Practicing TM reminds me of visiting Hindu temples as a kid and noticing how priests and worshippers alike would chant a single syllable: Om. A sound with a complex meaning; the whole universe coalesced into a single note. It doesn't matter whether you appreciate that or not. According to the TM practice, the sound is meaningless, nothing more than a vehicle to help the mind settle down. TM preaches by focusing exclusively on your mantra, you can reach higher states of consciousness and stillness. It also encourages thoughts to appear and disappear, like bubbles bursting in and out of existence.

While TM may be practiced differently than other forms of meditation, the goal is the same: training yourself to recognize negative or unwanted thought patterns and letting them go. Just recognizing mental models is a gargantuan task, as Mark explains:

We don't necessarily know our mental models...in User Experience design often what you do is you interview people who do the kind of work you want to support with a new [product], and they'll tell you what they do and the order they do things in. That helps gather what they consciously think they do, but then you also have to actually observe them doing what they do. Sometimes you'll

*realize what they think they do and what they actually
do are different. They might think they do all their work
on the computer, but when you go to observe what they do,
they have a little pad, paper, and pen they didn't mention
to you.*

Mark's experiences underscore the difficulty with uncovering
ingrained thought patterns and understandings. Thankfully,
though, meditation is a great, free tool we can implement to
help train our ability to detect them. Crucially as well, meditation is one of few ways we can discover and mitigate the ultimate mental model: the Ego. It's the ultimate mental model
because it's the most difficult to unmask. After all, aren't we
supposed to think and act with our self-interest in mind? Our
Ego, or the illusion of a sense of self experiencing the world, is
extremely adaptive, driving our ambition and survival.

But as Mark mentions,

> *The Ego is a construct. It's a mental model.... So, who
> is the experiencer? Is it your Ego or your consciousness?
> And the Ego evolves over time, but consciousness stays the
> same.... It's a question of what do we identify with? Pure
> consciousness—the witness of all activity—or Ego, a sense
> of self we give ourselves? So, I'm a seventy-three-year-old
> UX designer who is a father, husband, and grew up in
> San Francisco. But who is it that experiences my life? That
> UX designer or the consciousness underlying all of those
> individual experiences?*

Mark underscores how the Ego is a mental model unconsciously shaping how we view ourselves and our place in the

world. But it's not the only perspective. Some, like Mark, believe life is interconnected even though it's experienced by distinct individuals. And so, killing the Ego, or dispelling the illusion of a sense of self, is shifting one of our deepest patterns of thinking. Meditation is one of few tools helping us in this battle. It's kind of like going to a mental model gym. Its benefits may be similar to psychedelics. In fact, recent research suggests the brain displays the same chaotic pattern of activity during meditation as it does during a psychedelic experience (Dolan 2020).

Meditation has officially gone mainstream. By some estimates there are more than 2,500 meditation studios in the US alone (LaRosa 2019). There's even a Netflix special about it: *Headspace Guide to Meditation.* As many as 500 million people practice it, hoping to stave off stress and stress-related health problems (Marquez 2022). Mindfulness meditation, in particular, has become more popular in recent years. The practice of mindful meditation involves sitting comfortably, focusing on your breathing, then bringing your mind's attention to the present without drifting into concerns about the past or future.

But, as is true for a number of other alternative therapies, much of the evidence to support meditation's effectiveness in promoting mental or physical health isn't quite up to snuff. Why? "First, many studies don't include a good control treatment to compare with mindful meditation. Second, the people most likely to volunteer for a meditation study are often already sold on meditation's benefits and so are more likely to report positive effects" (Corliss 2014).

That all changed when researchers from Johns Hopkins University sifted through over nineteen thousand meditation studies. They found that mindful meditation can help ease psychological stresses like anxiety, depression, and pain. Dr. Elizabeth Hoge, a psychiatrist at the Center for Anxiety and Traumatic Stress Disorders at Massachusetts General Hospital, says mindfulness meditation makes perfect sense for treating anxiety.

"People with anxiety have a problem dealing with distracting thoughts that have too much power," she explains (Corliss 2014). "They can't distinguish between a problem-solving thought and a nagging worry that has no benefit" (Corliss 2014). "If you have unproductive worries," says Dr. Hoge, you can train yourself to experience those thoughts completely differently. "You might think 'I'm late, I might lose my job if I don't get there on time, and it will be a disaster!' Mindfulness teaches you to recognize, 'Oh, there's that thought again. I've been here before. But it's just that—a thought, and not a part of my core self'" (Corliss 2014).

One of her studies (which was included in the *JAMA Internal Medicine* review), found that a "mindfulness-based stress reduction program helped quell anxiety symptoms in people with generalized anxiety disorder, a condition marked by hard-to-control worries, poor sleep, and irritability" (Corliss 2014). Other studies indicate meditation is an effective tool to reduce symptoms of PTSD (Hopwood and Schutte 2017).

In my own life, I've discovered that meditating for ten to fifteen minutes each morning really helps me stay positive for the rest of my day. By training myself to acknowledge and let go of thoughts, I've prevented myself from spiraling into negativity whenever unpleasant thoughts emerge.

But meditation isn't without its risks or its challenges. Similar to psychedelics, it might be best to meditate under the guidance of a teacher or an app with recorded narration. In fact, researchers in one study found about 8 percent of people who try meditation experience an unwanted effect, ranging from an increase in anxiety to panic attacks (Wilson 2020).

That being said, Keri's experience, and recent research, make a compelling case for meditating as a way to recognize harmful or negative patterns of thinking. Consider giving meditation, whatever form makes the most sense for you, a try to help shed light on stealthy mental models.

CBT: THOUGHT PATTERN THERAPY

"Watch your thoughts, they become words. Watch your words, they become actions. Watch your actions, they become habits. Watch your habits, they become your character. Watch your character, it becomes your destiny."

—*Author Unknown*

Melissa Rivera always turned off the cameras before she binged. Newly married to a man who traveled frequently, the twenty-three-year-old med student would often comfort herself with food. Each time, she turned off the house's security system so her husband wouldn't see the coping mechanism she'd used since she was eight years old.

"I'd get this whole pizza that I would eat myself," she says. "At some point, I realized, 'This is killing me. I cannot do it anymore'" (Zulkey 2017). She sought help from counselors at the University of Texas, where she was a student.

Melissa suffered from binge eating disorder (BED), but the school's experts couldn't help. She says a school dietitian encouraged the very behavior that kicks off the binging cycle: restriction. "You have to eat so many grams of meat, you have to eat at most a cube of cheese per day," Melissa recalls the dietitian telling her (Zulkey 2017). Naturally, Melissa never followed that advice. Finally, at the end of 2016, she searched online and connected with Ed Tyson, a local eating-disorder specialist who practices cognitive behavioral therapy (CBT).

Unlike other forms of therapy, CBT is a specialized form of psychotherapeutic treatment that helps people learn how to identify and change destructive or disturbing thought patterns that have a negative influence on behavior and emotions.

CBT focuses on changing the automatic negative thoughts, a result of sticky mental models, that can contribute to and worsen emotional difficulties, depression, and anxiety. Practitioners of CBT argue that these spontaneous negative thoughts have a detrimental influence on mood, and the goal of treatment is to identify, challenge, and replace these thoughts with more objective, realistic thoughts. In other words, CBT aims to shift one's ingrained patterns of thinking and behaving to improve well-being.

At the time, Melissa knew little about CBT. After years of struggle and disappointment, she was skeptical about how much Ed could help. "Everything sounded like a beautiful promise, but it seemed impossible that he'd get me to this nice place that he was talking about," Melissa says (Zulkey 2017).

One out of every thirty-five adults suffer from BED, almost twice the combined rate for anorexia and bulimia (Bell 2015). It's characterized by repeated episodes of eating large quantities of food quickly and to the point of discomfort, a feeling of a loss of control during the binge, and guilt following the binge but without any consistent purging behavior. The good news is that BED is highly treatable, particularly with the help of cognitive behavioral therapy (CBT): nearly 80 percent of patients abstain from bingeing after twenty sessions (Zulkey 2017). And, unlike most calorie-restricting diets, the success of CBT holds for many patients over time. Melissa found great success with catching your thoughts, a CBT technique we'll explore further in a moment.

I'm happy to say despite her skepticism, Ed made good on that beautiful promise: Melissa has been binge-free for over a year.

The core principle driving CBT is the insight that our thoughts result in feelings leading to undesirable outcomes and behaviors. By that same logic, when someone changes their thoughts, it follows that they will also change their emotions and behaviors. We're typically aware of the outcomes of our feelings and thoughts, whether it's anxiety, pain or depression, but the key challenge is to reframe our thinking and address the cognitive distortions that prevent us from doing so.

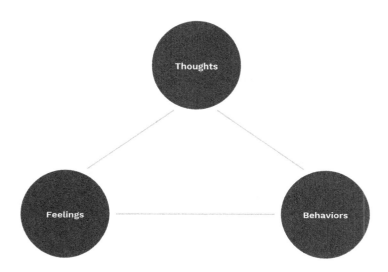

The CBT Cognitive Triangle

Dr. Klaybor, a specialist who has been treating patients with CBT techniques for over twenty years, mentions:

> *I flush out the negative thoughts and feelings and teach [them] how to reframe and address issues that prevent them from doing so.... In fact, I have a picture of one of my patients from fifteen years ago who was lying down while getting a vaccine with a thumbs up and a big smile. That came out of our work helping him [with his needle phobia] through CBT. This guy would [look at a needle and] pass out! He was a Stanford grad and on the football team, but if you showed him a needle he'd be out like a light. So, I actually went with him fifteen years ago to his doctor, taught him the techniques, was there to guide him through the vaccination, and it was successful.*

By recognizing and shifting one's thought patterns, amazing things like overcoming phobias and addressing disorders are within reach. But how does CBT accomplish this, and what can we learn? Taking a step back, it's helpful to note that CBT is based on several core principles, including:

1. Psychological problems are based, in part, on faulty or unhelpful ways of thinking (mental models).
2. Psychological problems are based, in part, on learned patterns of unhelpful behavior (results of mental models).
3. People suffering from psychological problems can learn better ways of coping with them (changing their mental models), thereby relieving their symptoms and becoming more effective in their lives.

That being said, CBT is not a magic bullet executing one's psychological problems, but it can help mitigate the influence our patterns of thinking have on our life and its overall quality.

It's striking how well aligned these principles are to the concept of mental models, including how we can never fully get rid of our mental models and the problems they create, but we can learn how to mitigate their influence. A few techniques we can borrow from CBT, which Dr. Klaybor graciously shared, to identify and change our thought patterns include:

1. **Thought Logs**—A daily journal of your thoughts to track your unconscious patterns of thinking, and focus on new ways of thinking to drill in. The main benefit is providing a way to capture thinking patterns (individual

and collections of thoughts over time) and the opportunity to revisit and revise them. Many common patterns like overgeneralizing, selective abstraction, or emotional reasoning lead to emotional problems both limiting and upsetting.

2. **Breath Control**—Methods to release tension and relax one's muscles, which over time modifies our reactions to stress. Progressive muscle relaxation (PMR) and abdominal breathing (AB) techniques help us reduce our body's need to activate the "fight or flight" response and to communicate safety to the brain.

3. **Mental Rehearsal**—We worry about things because we *feel* like we're not fully prepared for them, even if we actually are. In its most basic form, mental rehearsal is a way to convince yourself you are prepared. It's the process of identifying the source of your worries, determining how you can adapt if things go bad, and practicing all your contingency plans in your mind until you feel so prepared that your worrying melts away. Mental rehearsal is a helpful way to direct anxiety and undesirable thoughts toward productive activity, even if it seems counter-intuitive to fight negative thoughts with more negative thoughts.

4. **Gratitude Journal**—The basic practice is straightforward: One simply needs to record three things they experienced in the past day or week for which they're grateful. The entries are supposed to be brief (just a single sentence), and they range from the mundane (waking up this morning) to the sublime (the generosity of friends) to the timeless (Tame Impala). Gratitude journals help reduce hopelessness, promote positive thinking, and increase overall gratitude; all of which are critical to avoid downward spirals.

5. **Catching Your Thoughts**—Recognizing when you have a thought, it is just a thought. We have a choice to either treat each thought as a truth or treat it as a lie. It's what you do after that helps make those decisions. If you have a random thought pop up, like "Am I that hungry," catching yourself would be realizing immediately after "No, I ate, I'm fulfilled. I don't need to act on that, I can throw [that thought] out and move on." The key here is to strip your thoughts of the power and control they normally have over you, preventing them from leading to feelings and undesirable outcomes or behaviors.

6. **Cognitive Restructuring**—Imagine it's your birthday. You're expecting a phone call from a close friend, but it never comes. You called them on *their* birthday, so why didn't they call you? Do they not care enough to remember your birthday? You feel hurt. Where did this feeling of hurt come from? It wasn't the lack of a phone call that caused the hurt. It was the *thoughts* about the lack of a phone call that hurt. What if, instead of taking the missing phone call personally, you had thought: "My friend is so forgetful! I bet they don't know anyone's birthday" or "maybe something came up unexpectedly, and they're busy." In other words, cognitive restructuring is the therapeutic process of identifying and challenging negative and irrational thoughts.

Revisiting Melissa's case, CBT techniques like thought logging can help patients suffering from BED identify episodes of over-restriction or under-restriction to encourage normal eating patterns. By catching one's thoughts and focusing on restructuring, patients can challenge harsh, stereotyped views of being overweight and promote acceptance of diverse body sizes. Mental rehearsal and breath control are powerful techniques to cope with high-risk situations and help with maintaining changes.

CBT isn't just for individuals. Dr. Klaybor recounted a story of a couple he worked with who were struggling with their marriage. After a few sessions digging into what was happening, he constructed a visual representation of the destructive, unconscious thought and behavior patterns they engaged in.

At first, their cycle of behavior looked like the following:

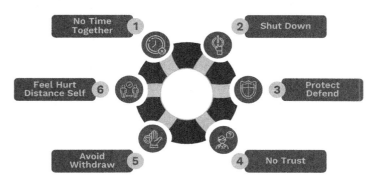

Without knowing it, the couple's mental model of their relationship was driving them apart. Because they didn't spend much time together, they shut down and became defensive. Over time, this eroded the trust they once developed and caused each of them to withdraw and distance themselves. Sadly, this would reinforce avoiding time together, and the pernicious cycle continued.

By leveraging some of the previously mentioned techniques—thought logs, gratitude journals, and breath control—the couple's relationship greatly improved. After several CBT sessions, the couple's pattern of thinking and behavior shifted toward a more positive cycle, shown below:

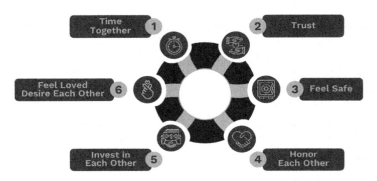

Thanks to CBT, the couple started spending time together, reinforcing the trust they have in one another. This virtuous cycle results in each person feeling safe, excited to honor and invest in each other, and ultimately desiring to be and spend time together. Now that the couple's mental models have shifted, they're a lot happier in their relationship.

The potential for CBT to improve lives is seemingly endless. The practice has been proven to treat a wide array of diseases, including irritable bowel syndrome, bulimia, and anxiety disorders to aiding in stress management (Murpy et al. 2010; Tang et al. 2013; Kaczkurkin and Foa 2015; Ghazavi et al. 2016). Unfortunately, while CBT is a powerful tool, access to therapy can be difficult given the limited number of trained therapists and the sizable, out-of-pocket expense. For those of us who can't see a trained therapist, adopting

CBT techniques that resonate may be the next best course of action.

Like psychedelic-assisted therapy and meditation, CBT is orders of magnitude more effective in the right settings with the right guidance. The built-in accountability of seeing someone and reporting your progress shouldn't be underestimated either.

The true power of CBT lies in its focus on exposing and shifting troublesome mental models. By challenging our existing ways of thinking, CBT enables us to find new paths. If your current mental models are limiting or harming your life, as Dr. Klaybor says, "What can you gain by losing your way?"

Mental models are complex, invisible filters shaping the way we think and behave. It should come as no surprise that exposing and changing them can be difficult. While there is no silver bullet, psychedelic-assisted therapy, meditation, and CBT are research-backed ways proven to help us in this long journey.

One or none of these may work for you, and it's important to make smart choices with your personal habits and tendencies in mind. For instance, if you generally feel anxious and find negative thoughts intruding whenever you pause to think, then meditation may not be helpful for you. But cognitive behavioral therapy with a licensed provider could be just what you need to help reframe your negative thought patterns. If you would be uncomfortable relinquishing control over your state of mind, psychedelics may not be for you. For others, though, psychedelic-assisted therapy can help induce tranquil states conducive to opening their minds to calmer or different patterns of thinking.

From my own experience, I recommend combining several of these approaches to achieve the strongest result. In cybersecurity, the concept of a layered defense is critical: incorporating and combining multiple tools greatly improves the security of the network against multiple threats. When it comes to shifting our patterns of thinking, a layered approach can be greatly beneficial as well.

For instance, psilocybin could be a second-line treatment for those who struggle with meditation. "Psilocybin can be a gateway into meditation...to show you experiences and to have insight into yourself," said Peter Addy from Yale University School of Medicine and founding member of the Yale Psychedelic Science Group (Senthilingam 2016). Similarly, CBT combined with psychedelic-assisted therapy, the model Rainfall Medicine is exploring, can be more effective than either are when administered separately. Ultimately, it's important to know yourself, your personal challenges or limitations, and try different techniques accordingly.

Never forget that, like the one-armed Judo champion, we can always turn our perceived weaknesses into strengths, and mental models are no exception.

Note: I don't profess to be an expert in meditation (although I've practiced daily for the past three years), CBT, or psychedelics (I've had my fair share of trips). There are many better books to read if you're looking for how to implement or try these activities. To learn more about psychedelics and how they work, I'd recommend How to Change Your Mind *by Michael Pollen, and for a practical meditation guide consider the book* The Mind Illuminated. *There's no way to practice CBT by yourself; for that, please go see a licensed therapist.*

Psychedelic Truths—Rohit Gupta

I can't seem to figure out my purpose,
But I want to change this never-ending circus.

It's easy to see that lack of love is what's at the core,
But when you follow the crowd you're always left
wanting more.

It's hard to embrace when you're so full of disgrace,
Maybe it's time to consider a trip to hyperspace.

Everyone agrees that there are plants that can heal,
But if you bring up psychedelics, it becomes quite
the ordeal.

Learning to love yourself can seem quite daring,
Especially when you have to face all of the pain you
are bearing.

If making others happy is how you choose to live out
your existence,
You will always have an acquaintance and no need for
resistance.

Try LSD under supervision and see,
You can shift your thought patterns and all the debris.

Paradigms shifting in front of awakening eyes,
Psychedelic truths hidden within the tides of time.

The Guest House—Jalaluddin Rumi

This being human is a guest house.
Every morning a new arrival.

A joy, a depression, a meanness,
some momentary awareness comes
as an unexpected visitor.

Welcome and entertain them all!
Even if they're a crowd of sorrows,
who violently sweep your house
empty of its furniture,
still, treat each guest honorably.
He may be clearing you out
for some new delight.

The dark thought, the shame, the malice,
meet them at the door laughing,
and invite them in.

Be grateful for whoever comes,
because each has been sent
as a guide from beyond.

Untitled—ACT Auntie

Thoughts and feelings arise and fall away,
Ebbing and flowing every day.

When we resist them,
We can get into trouble.

Trying to avoid them?
Make that double!

Instead can you be willing to just let them be?
Accept them as normal and natural as the sea.

Yes sometimes it will be stormy,
Sometimes it will be calm,

But thoughts are just thoughts,
They cannot do you any harm.

Imagine hearing them on a radio or said in a silly voice,
You don't have to take them so seriously…you always have
a choice!

Instead put your energy into who you want to be,
What do you want to stand for, ask "what matters to me?"

Follow your values and learn to float, sail, and surf,
Create a life you love, full of meaning and worth!

REFLECTIONS

- Psychedelic substances are often thought of as party drugs or dangerous to use. Does a greater understanding of their potential therapeutic benefits change how you view them? Would you ever consider trying psychedelic substances in controlled settings?
- Have you ever tried meditation? If so, what worked for you, and what didn't? Is there a form of meditation—TM, instructor-led, etc.—you'd be willing to try to help you become more aware of your thoughts?
- What's a weakness of yours that may actually be a strength? How can you shift your mindset to achieve that?

EXERCISES

- Choose a pattern of behavior you've been trying to change (examples can include negativity, relationship challenges, or dealing with anxious thoughts). Now, create a CBT cycle explaining how that pattern plays out to the ones Dr. Klaybor constructed for the couple he was advising. What are some ways you can shift that cycle to reach a more positive outcome?
- This exercise is a staple of mindfulness, designed to simply enhance your awareness of your own thoughts. To begin, sit or lie down in a comfortable position and try to let all tension in your body dissipate. Focus on your breathing first, then move your awareness to what it feels like to be in your body, and finally move on to your thoughts. Be aware of what comes into your head but resist the urge to label or judge these thoughts.

- Think of them as a passing cloud in the sky of your mind. If your mind wanders to chase a thought, acknowledge whatever it was that took your attention and gently guide your attention back to your thoughts. Take ten minutes to complete this exercise and reflect on how you can catch your thoughts to prevent them from leading to unwanted feelings and behaviors.

• When we listen to another person, we choose whether we agree with what they have to say (or not). With our internal voice, we don't usually feel like we have that option to agree or disagree, but that's the posture I'd like you to try taking. Research has shown that naming your mind—give it a name other than the one you call yourself—helps with this. Why? Because if your mind has a different name, it is different from "you." I call mine "George." Pick any name you like; even Mr. Mind or Ms. Mind will do.

- Now say hello to your mind by using its new name, as if you were being introduced to it at a party. Of course, if you are around others while you're reading this—say, on a bus or a train—do this in your head. As you listen to your thoughts and notice when your mind starts to chatter, answer it back with something like, "Thanks for that thought, George. Really, thank you." If you speak to your mind dismissively, it will continue right on problem-solving, so be sincere. You might want to add, "I really get that you're trying to be of use, so thank you for that. But I've got this covered." Say this out loud if you're alone, or internally if you're with others.

– Your mind will probably push back with thoughts like, "That's silly! That won't help!" Respond again with, "Thanks for that thought, George. Thank you. I really do see how you are trying to be of use." You might consider inviting it to comment further by replying, "Got anything else you have to say?"

Mental Food for Model Thoughts

"I can only show you the door, you're the one that has to walk through it."

The agents, sensing an imminent threat, turn around and lay eyes on their mortal enemy. Instinctively, they fire. And keep firing. With a barrage of bullets hurtling toward him, Neo steadfastly raises his hand.

At the very last moment, a miracle happens: the bullets are robbed of their motion, frozen in time.

Neo finally sees The Matrix for what it is: millions of lines of code and patterns manifesting as programs.

While it took Neo the length of an entire movie to experience his epiphany, don't be surprised if it takes you months or even years to recognize and shift your mental models. After all, the difficult exercise we're engaging in requires using your brain to unravel how your brain is working.

Unlike Neo, I doubt you'll see code everywhere you go, but don't be surprised if you start noticing mental models and their influence in your own life, others' lives, and society at large. Remember that mental models are just deeply held patterns of thinking based on beliefs, not facts. We saw this exemplified in chapter two, where the mental model cycle caused folks like Charles in Group A and others in Group B to have radically different responses to the COVID-19 pandemic. Do you recognize any unconscious opinions, biases, or beliefs in your life which followed a similar path? In relationships, at work, or in your community?

Mental models, like all of us, are neither good nor bad. Rather, they're a shade of gray, which at times act as incredible tools underpinning our ability to recognize patterns, solve problems, and work well as a team in high-pressure situations. But just like the story of Cassandra cautions—the Trojan princess gifted with prophetic sight but cursed to never be believed—each of these gifts comes with a price: seeing patterns where there are none, innovation inertia, and maintaining social boundaries. The stories we often unknowingly tell ourselves can be forces for good or chaos, but it all depends on how we decide to leverage them.

Applying a mental model lens to a host of events and situations—from Chrysler's massive recall to the difficulty of helping small family farms—reveals how any behavior change requires an understanding of mental models to succeed. Perhaps you'll start noticing physical objects seem poorly or superbly designed, depending on whether they were made with an understanding of users' mental models in mind. Or how local initiatives like bag taxes won't actually change people's use of plastic bags outside of grocery stores, because our patterns of thinking normalized using them long ago.

In your own life, the next time you feel the influence of caste identity or try to unlearn an undesirable habit, recall that mental models naturally make it difficult. It's not your fault any change will take time, but it simply means you need to shift your ingrained patterns of thinking. We don't struggle to lose weight or overcome an addiction because we aren't trying hard enough, but because we haven't reframed the patterns which enable these undesired behaviors. If you ever unconsciously avoid people you associate with danger, know you're not a bad person. Your mental models just need work, and it's up to you to change them.

Beyond the obvious benefits, shifting our patterns of thinking can provide other incredible superpowers. They may not be the ones you were hoping for as a kid, but the ability to understand and learn from those who disagree with us and the clarity needed to live a more fulfilling life are arguably some of the most meaningful. Imagine if you could make peace with your irritable parent, who you just can't see eye-to-eye with, or if you could change your work habits to get a better response from your supervisor and rise up the career ladder faster, or find the breakthrough on that project you've been stuck on for months.

If you're ever frustrated by a mental model you uncover and want to change, don't despair. Help is here and readily available in the form of psychedelic-assisted therapy, meditation, cognitive behavioral therapy, and journaling. Please just make sure to only seek assistance from licensed and trained professionals; otherwise, you risk making matters worse.

Keep in mind that the key to identifying mental models is continuously and consciously holding a mirror to ourselves (whether through introspection, journaling, meditation, or other methods) to uncover ways of thinking of which we aren't consciously aware.

Shifting mental models might be even more difficult, akin to changing out all the standard utensils in your home for chopsticks. Even those who grew up using these unparalleled utensils would struggle to unlearn how to cut using a knife, and then learn how to slice with chopsticks instead.

But over time, despite how frustrating it may be, you'll slowly forget you even used knives to cut, once using chopsticks becomes second-nature. Similarly, it's critical to practice a habit of mental model introspection until doing so becomes second-nature. Only through training, accountability, and holding a mirror to ourselves can we see our mental models for what they really are: beliefs shaping our behavior, actions, and ways of understanding things.

A world in which people take time to expose and change their mental models is one where unconscious bias and its deadly repercussions are drastically reduced, people are empowered to pursue what they're truly passionate about, and innovation isn't impeded by ingrained ways of thinking. In this brave new world, we'll work together more effectively than ever before, put aside our differences and learn from one another, and align our unconscious thoughts and actions with our values.

If nothing else, I hope reading *The Invisible Filter* imparts an appreciation for the influence mental models have on your life and instills a sense of confidence that you can do something about it—if you choose to. Like Neo in *The Matrix* and Ashitaka in *Princess Mononoke*, I hope the journey you persevere through enables you to look past the filter, with eyes unclouded by your patterns of thinking.

Mental models are all around us. Even now, in this very room. You can see them when you look out your window or when you turn on your television. You'll feel their presence when you go to work, to church, and when you pay your taxes.

"It is the world that has been pulled over your eyes, to blind you from the truth."
— *The Matrix* (MOVIECLIPS 2011)

The truth is you aren't truly free. You never have been. Like everyone else, your thoughts and actions have been shaped by a filter you cannot see or touch: your mental models. Thankfully, though, not all hope is lost. You can expose, change, and leverage these patterns of thinking, and in the process gain superpowers, but only if you consciously and continuously hold a mirror to yourself.

Unfortunately, I have nothing left to teach and share with you. And, frankly speaking, it's impossible to *fully* appreciate mental models by reading about them. You have to see, reflect on, and experience them for yourself.

"This is your last chance. After this, there's no turning back."
— *The Matrix* (MOVIECLIPS 2011)

Now, at the end of our adventure, I have something to give you. In my left hand is a red pill. In my right hand a blue one. You take the blue pill and the journey ends—you'll go back to your existing life, thinking and acting however your mental models guide you. But if you take the red pill, you'll head toward this unpredictable, exciting place where your life will be quite different. Free from the shackles of your ingrained ways of thinking, you can build yourself anew.

Only you can see how deep the rabbit hole goes.

So, what will it be?

Loop—Afiyah the Poet

Stuck in the endless spiral
my mind loops in the familiar

I've been here
many times before
with patterns drawn
for the universe to see

same lines
same place
I see the progression

Riding this takes me
to the same old place

despair
hopelessness
questions unanswered

Staying on makes for
a predictable path

This loop has no
ending or beginning

Just the same route
in perpetual repeat

Let me slide off
this loop of hell

And let me find
the peace I'm looking for.

Climate Thoughts & Patterns

*"The climate crisis has already been solved.
We already have the facts and solutions. All
we have to do is wake up and change."*

—GRETA THUNBERG

Before you go, let me leave you with a real example of how understanding and shifting mental models helped me change my life. At the same time, we'll explore how to use the concepts this book introduces in a meaningful way: aligning disparate mental models to make real progress with climate change—a tall task, no doubt.

If you're reading this book, I don't need to tell you that climate change is real. Whether it's record-breaking temperatures, strange weather fluctuations, stronger storms, or an increase in flooding, the effects of climate change are impossible to ignore. Despite a lot of conversation and outrage from youth and environmental groups, we haven't done much about it in the United States. In fact, research conducted by the Rhodium Group demonstrates that while some industries like power generation have made significant strides in reducing emissions, many other sectors including buildings, transportation, and agriculture haven't materially changed their emissions since 2005 (Milman 2022; Congressional Research Service 2021).

Why?

It's not because we lack the necessary technology, nor is it due to a lack of awareness; the real issue at play is folks are unable to change their ingrained ways of thinking and behavior, preventing us from working together to make a meaningful difference.

I know firsthand just how difficult it is to reframe mental models, especially those related to climate change. Because these mental models are tied to behaviors we never typically question—eating meat, traveling, using electricity, appreciating nature as it exists today—they can be incredibly difficult to uncover and change. Maybe that's why my journey to renouncing meat and adopting vegetarianism as a sophomore in college was several years in the making.

For as long as I can remember, I've been obsessed with animals. My first animal fascination was with dinosaurs at the tender age of five. I knew the names of many different species by heart and couldn't resist playing with the Mattel dinosaur action figures my parents bought me. Fast forward a few years (when

I was old enough to watch TV) and I was helplessly glued to Discovery Channel and Animal Planet because I loved learning about new species of animals and cool animal facts.

For instance, did you know the duck-billed platypus is just one of two mammals (the other one is the echidna) to lay eggs? Ten-year-old me thought that was absolutely bonkers; admittedly, I still do. Encountering a myriad of birds, dogs, cats, oaks, and insects as I hiked in the Sierra Azul Open Space Preserve near my home only reinforced the appreciation I had for other forms of life.

That all being said, I loved to eat chicken. Whether it was chicken tenders or chicken tikka, I don't think a single day passed by from the ages of ten to eighteen where I didn't eat chicken in some form. It never occurred to me that chickens were beautiful creatures deserving love and respect, despite feeling that way about other forms of life we haven't arbitrarily deemed "food."

My first wake-up call that the mental models I formed about meat weren't aligned with my values came in high school. You see, I attended a Jesuit, all-male high school which firmly believed in molding its students to become "men for others." Naturally, the school devoted one week out of every year to teach its rather sheltered boys about social justice issues and the darkness existing in the real world. One of the key issues we learned about was the food industry's inhumane treatment of animals.

Until this point, I was blissfully ignorant of how the chicken I loved eating came to be. After all, the meat industry spends millions on marketing and advertisements designed to mislead us. For instance, a carton of "all natural" eggs might bear an illustration of a rustic farm, packages of chicken meat are often touted as "humanely raised," and milk ads make it seem like dairy cows have great lives. In a few cases, these sunny depictions are accurate. But far too often they mask the industrial conditions under which these animals were raised, abused, and slaughtered.

Animal welfare and consumer protection advocates have a name for such misleading labeling: "humanewashing." Research suggests it's having precisely the effect meat producers intend it to. A recent national survey by C.O.nxt, a food marketing firm, found animal welfare and "natural" claims on meat, dairy, and egg packaging increased the intent to purchase for over half of consumers.

The humanewashing campaigns certainly worked on me. I never once questioned the treatment of the animals I consumed. But all of that changed when one of my teachers played a short documentary called *Meet Your Meat*, created by the nonprofit organization People for the Ethical Treatment of Animals (PETA), which details several cases of animal cruelty within the meat industry.

Some of the material covered in *Meet Your Meat* includes:

- Egg-laying hens live in crowded cages, six or seven hens to one battery cage the size of a file drawer.
- Cattle are castrated, their horns removed, and third-degree burns (livestock branding) are inflicted on them, all without anesthetic.

- Cows used for their milk have calves removed from them shortly after birth. These calves are sent to veal farms.
- Chickens bred and drugged to grow so quickly that their hearts, lungs, and limbs often can't keep up.
- Mother pigs (sows) are confined to gestation crates so small that the pigs cannot turn around or even lie down.

It was absolutely heart-wrenching to see this firsthand, and I could feel my stomach twisting knowing I was blindly supporting these gruesome practices. What bothered me most, however, was realizing that my ignorance was truthfully no one's fault but my own; I just accepted the narratives spoon-fed to me when skepticism was certainly warranted. Sadly, it took all of ten minutes for those feelings to subside; when class ended, I promptly grabbed another chicken sandwich for lunch from the neighborhood deli and reactivated familiar mental models, which minimized the issues at hand.

Shifting the mental models I formed about how the animals I ate were being treated wouldn't be easy. Only several years later—after watching many more documentaries, experiencing how life is interconnected through psychedelic trips, and learning more about meat's impact on our health—did I give up eating meat for good.

Changing and challenging my food habits was my gateway to understanding climate change and how I can make a difference in my daily life, but it took a *long* time. So, when I read about how individuals struggle to accept the reality of climate change, which requires reframing ingrained ways of thinking, I empathize rather than judge.

There's no better example of mental model-induced climate denial than the real-estate agents of Miami.

MIAMI'S CLIMATE DENIAL

The sea level in Miami has risen ten inches since 1900; in the two thousand years prior, it barely changed (Loria 2018). The consensus among informed observers is that the sea will rise in Miami Beach somewhere between thirteen and thirty-four inches by 2050 (Miller 2019). By 2100, it is extremely likely to be closer to six feet, which means, unless you own a yacht and a helicopter, *sayonara*.

What makes Miami exceptionally vulnerable to climate change is its unique geology. The city—and its satellite towns and resort—is built on a dome of porous limestone which is soaking up the rising seawater, slowly filling up the city's foundations and then bubbling up through drains and pipes. Miami's low topography only adds to these problems. "There is little land out here that rises more than six feet above sea level. Many condos and apartment blocks open straight on the edge of the sea. Of the total of 4.2 million US citizens who live at an elevation of four feet or less, 2.4 million of them live in south Florida" (McKie 2014).

At Florida International University, geologist Peter Harlem created a series of maps charting what will happen as the sea continues to rise. These show that by the time oceans have risen by four feet (a fairly conservative forecast), most of Miami Beach, Key Biscayne, Virginia Key, and the area's other pieces of prime real estate will be bathtubs. "At six feet,

Miami's waterfront and the Florida Keys will have disappeared" (McKie 2014).

Miami is facing a calamity worthy of the Old Testament. Despite its vast wealth, the city might soon be consumed by the sea. But what really surprises visitors and observers is the city's response, or rather, it's almost total lack of reaction. The local population is steadily increasing, land prices continue to surge, and building is progressing at a healthy pace. During my own visit in December 2021, signs of construction (new shopping malls, cranes towering over new condominiums and scaffolding enclosing freshly built apartment blocks) could be seen across the city, its backers apparently oblivious of scientists' warnings that the foundations of their buildings may be awash very soon.

Sarah Miller, a writer and editor for the journalist-owned magazine *Popula*, wanted to explore this widespread cognitive dissonance for herself. She posed as a prospective home buyer to speak with local real-estate agents and understand their ways of thinking.

Sarah asked one agent, a tall and fair man of possibly Swedish origins, how the flooding was. "There are pump stations everywhere, and the roads were raised" he said (Miller 2019). "So that's all been fixed" (Miller 2019). She followed up by asking how the hurricanes were. He shared that because the hurricanes came from the tropics, from the south and this was the west side of Miami Beach, they were not that bad in this neighborhood. "Oh, right," Sarah said, as if that made any sense (Miller 2019).

Bluntly, Sarah asked, "They're not worried about sea level rise?"

The agent quipped back, "It's definitely something the city is trying to combat. They are fighting it, by raising everything. But so far, it hasn't been an issue" (Miller 2019).

She couldn't wait to steal this line, slightly altered. "I am afraid of dying, sure, but so far, it hasn't been an issue" (Miller 2019).

The next real estate agent was much more charming than the first. "She was in her mid-forties, in heels and slacks so perfectly tailored she looked like she'd been sewn into them. Her tan ring finger was graced with some bright gem, surrounded by diamonds, and big enough to plate a filet mignon" (Miller 2019).

When asked about whether sea level rise concerns her, the agent replied, "The scientists, economists, and environmentalists that are saying this stuff, they don't realize what a wealthy area this is" (Miller 2019). She noted that she lived here and wasn't leaving, and the people selling Miami were all working on the same goal as a community to maintain this place, with the pumps, zoning and raising the streets. Apparently, there were just too many millionaires and billionaires here for a disaster on a great scale to be allowed to take place.

Another agent, when asked about the impacts of climate change, mentioned Amsterdam and how they were *making it work*.

But there are several problems with comparing Miami to the Netherlands.

> *One of these is that Amsterdam has spent billions of dollars on climate change and Miami has spent millions. The Dutch strategy is holistic, looking at how this thing will affect that thing, etc., whereas in Miami they have just installed some pumps and raised roads and buildings, which kind of neglects to consider that a place to live is really only useful insofar as nearby goods and services, and roads, are not underwater (Miller 2019).*

Again, I share these examples not to shame or cast judgment on the individuals mentioned but to convey how difficult it is to confront and change ways of thinking related to climate change. It's evident the human mind isn't wired to prioritize seemingly abstract, long-term consequences over short-term pleasures. Nor was it designed to embrace change. That none of the agents Sarah spoke with ever acknowledged the timing and severity of climate change's effects—despite plenty of evidence to the contrary—suggests that ill-informed mental models are to blame.

Our collective ability to combat climate change rests on our individual capacity to understand and reframe climate misaligned ways of thinking. But it's one thing to appreciate that others' ways of thinking prevent them from taking climate action or preparing for its impacts, and another matter altogether to shift them. However, that's precisely what we need to do to protect ourselves from climate change's immediate impacts and prevent them from getting worse.

CHANGING CLIMATE THOUGHT PATTERNS

When we encounter folks who have different mental models than we do, we can't throw studies and facts at them; if that worked, they wouldn't think the way they do. Instead, we need to reframe our messages with their patterns of thinking in mind. Specifically, we need to:

1. **Lead with values, not facts.** According to Dr. Hayhoe, a climate scientist at Texas Tech University and an evangelical Christian, if you want to convince someone about climate change, don't lead with data. In her experience, Dr. Hayhoe has found the best way to neutralize the partisan charge on climate change is not by appealing to science—which some prominent Republicans, such as Senator Ted Cruz, have cast as a competitor to religion—but by emphasizing shared values. "For some, this could be the well-being of our community," she writes (Bokat-Lindell 2020). "For others, our children, and for fellow Christians, it's often our faith" (Bokat-Lindell 2020). For example, research has found that Conservatives are more likely to support a pro-environmental agenda when presented with messages containing themes of patriotism and defending the purity of nature (Wolsko et al. 2016).

2. **Emphasize the potential benefits instead of focusing on harms.** For many skeptics, delineating the myriad potential harms of unmitigated climate change is not an effective strategy. A comprehensive study published in *Nature* in 2015 surveyed six thousand people across twenty-four countries and found that emphasizing the shared benefits of climate change was an effective way

of motivating people to take action—even if they initially identified as deniers (Bain et al. 2015). For example, people were more likely to take steps to mitigate climate change if they believe it will produce economic and scientific development. Most importantly, these results were true across political ideology, age, and gender.

3. **Recognize that the messenger matters.** Who makes for the best messenger depends, naturally, on the intended recipient. A study published in *Nature* in 2019, for example, found that when it comes to parents, children may be especially effective persuaders: because climate change perceptions in children seem less susceptible to the influence of worldview or political context, it may be possible for them to inspire adults toward higher levels of climate concern, and in turn, collective action (Lawson et al. 2019). Child-to-parent intergenerational learning— that is, the transfer of knowledge, attitudes or behaviors from children to parents—may be a promising pathway to overcoming socio-ideological barriers to climate concern.

There's unfortunately no silver bullet to shift others' mental models, and we can all appreciate how difficult it is to even just change our own patterns of thinking. But to make progress we need to tailor our approach to skeptics' mental models, rather than framing our messages in a way that appeals to our ways of thinking.

If I could go back in time and speak with my younger self, I'd emphasize the benefits of reducing meat consumption and illustrate how my food choices at the time weren't aligned with my actual values. There's no way to know if that would've made a difference, but I can imagine it would've at least inspired me to understand whether my ways of thinking were actually serving me.

My hope is reading *The Invisible Filter* motivates you to undertake a similar journey. You can get started by 1) taking time to uncover your ingrained ways of thinking, 2) examining whether those mental models align with your values and goals, and 3) working diligently to shift and reframe your misaligned thought patterns.

While our fates and our planet's destiny are uncertain, challenging the stories we unknowingly tell ourselves is the first step we can take to ensure they are futures worth fighting for.

Acknowledgments

Thank you to everyone who has been a part of my journey writing *The Invisible Filter*. If you read all the way through this book to the end and have landed on this page, you should be acknowledged. Writing this book was quite a journey; it almost didn't happen dozens of times. My biggest accomplishment was sitting still long enough to get these thoughts out of my head and onto a laptop, typically following busy workdays. Doing so meant being quieter and more absent than usual in the lives of loved ones. To my friends and family who encouraged my writing process, edited my words, and discussed related topics every step of the way, I am forever grateful.

I need to thank my life partner and best friend, Sabrina Sukumar, for giving me the time and emotional support I needed to tell this story. You had a front-row seat to all the insecurities, procrastination, and long nights. There would be no book without your patience and love.

Ramesh and Sunitha, you were the first people who made room for me to dare, regardless of what it cost or the stress it brought you. Thanks for being my amazing parents and champions since day one.

My dear beta readers—Ed, Elaine, James, Sabrina, Savan, and Varun—I had some nerve asking you to read my whole book and give comments when most of you were busy with work or recruiting! Thanks for always making me better. I couldn't have done this without you, and I wouldn't dare try.

To the team at the Creator Institute and New Degree Press, thank you for providing a platform to bring my book to life. Eric Koester, Brian Bies, Mike Butler, and Olivia Bearden deserve special thanks. Mike and Olivia are the heroes of this publishing story. Thanks for your calming presence, your sharp eye, your steady commitment to keeping me accountable to myself, and your constant reassurance.

Thank you to my interviewees—without you, there would be no book. Each of your stories are a testament of your strength, resilience, and courage. In addition to those who have chosen to remain anonymous, thank you to the following individuals for your expertise and stories:

- Dr. Alexandra Mack
- Dr. Michael Klaybor
- Divya Gupta
- Mark Lubeck
- Paola Betchart

This book was made possible also by a community of people who believed in me so fervently they preordered their copies and helped promote the book before it even went to print. Thanks to you all, many of whom read my early manuscript and gave input on the book title and cover. You are amazing!

Here are all my supporters listed in alphabetical order by first name:

Abimbola Adegbulu
Aditya Kotecha
Ajay Ghai
Ajay Shanmugham
Amidhara Desai
Anish Kumar Sinha
Anupama Donthi
Aston Pierce
Avantika Molugu
Blake Pennington
Caley Zheng
Chris Langland
Christopher Kim
Connie Qian
Connor Mullaney
David Laszlo
Davis Auksmuksts
Dhanya Madhusudan
Divya Gupta
Edward Kim
Elias Can
Elizabeth Mossessian
Eric Koester
Ernie Bio
Everett Young
Fausto Lendeborg
George Damouny
Hiroto Udagawa
Ishan Sinha

Jacob Hands
James Buckel
Jeffrey Gantner
Jerry Wu
Julie Li
Katrina Cockrell
Krishna Kumar
Latha Krishnamurthi
Lawrence Han
Lisa Lee
Manoj Ahluwalia
Martin Sajon
Masaki Noguchi
Matthew Claxton
Maxim Baban
Mercy Caprara
Michael Leffer
Murali Joshi
Nandika Donthi
Navsher Singh
Nick Chow
Pranay Singal
Radha Verma
Rak Garg
Ramesh Gupta
Rick Tacelli
Sabrina Sukumar
Sachidanand Vrindavanam
Savan Patel

Shawn Samra
Shiraz Kazmi
Shyamala Kumar
Sneha Vankamamidi
Sonali Kalje
Stephan Liu
Sukumar Subburayan
Sushmita Datta

Uday Molugu
Vandana Bhanoori
Varsha Praveen
Vashti Srinivas
Visweswara Mocherla
William Lin
Yair Solow
Zuk Avraham

Glossary

THE JOURNEY

- Balk: To refuse abruptly; to stop short and refuse to proceed
- Depth charges: An antisubmarine weapon that consists essentially of a drum filled with explosives which is dropped near a target and descends to a predetermined depth where it explodes
- Incommunicado: Without means of communication; in a situation or state not allowing communication
- Innocuous: Not likely to give offense or to arouse strong feelings or hostility
- Transfix: To hold motionless by or as if by piercing

WHAT'S A MENTAL MODEL?

- Dopamine: A neurotransmitter that plays a role in how we feel pleasure and is released when your brain is expecting a reward
- Übermensch: Overman; meant to be an ideal future human and an ultimate goal for humanity

BENEFITS & DRAWBACKS

- Antagonism: Actively expressed opposition or hostility
- Enjoin: To direct or impose by authoritative order or with urgent admonition
- Heikegani: A species of crab native to Japan, with a shell that bears a pattern resembling a human face which many believed to be the face of an angry samurai hence the nickname samurai crab
- Pareidolia: The tendency to perceive a specific, often meaningful image in a random or ambiguous visual pattern
- Precocious: Exhibiting mature qualities at an unusually early age

TO CHANGE OR NOT TO CHANGE?

- Adage: A saying often in metaphorical form that typically embodies a common observation
- Eurocentric: Reflecting a tendency to interpret the world in terms of European or Anglo-American values and experiences
- Mestizo: Any person of mixed blood; in Central and South America it denotes a person of combined Indian and European extraction
- Upend: To affect to the point of being upset or flurried; overturn

WHY APPLY

- Caste: One of the hereditary social classes in Hinduism restricting the occupation of their members and their association with the members of other castes; a division of society based on differences of wealth, inherited rank or privilege, profession, occupation, or race
- Platitudes: A remark or statement, especially one with a moral content, that has been used too often to be interesting or thoughtful

SUPERPOWERS

- Biopower: [A] power that exerts a positive influence on life, that endeavors to administer, optimize, and multiply it, subjecting it to precise controls and comprehensive regulations
- Uighur: A member of a Turkic people powerful in Mongolia and eastern Turkestan between the eighth and twelfth centuries AD who constitute a majority of the population of Chinese Turkestan

ALTER, DON'T FALTER

- Apocryphal: Of doubtful authenticity
- Ayahuasca: A psychoactive beverage containing dimethyltryptamine prepared especially from the bark of a woody vine (*Banisteriopsis caapi* of the family Malpighiaceae) and the leaves of a shrubby plant (*Psychotria viridis* of the family Rubiaceae) of South America

- Bulimia: A serious eating disorder that occurs chiefly in females, is characterized by compulsive overeating usually followed by self-induced vomiting or laxative or diuretic abuse, and is often accompanied by guilt and depression
- Ego death: The (often instantaneous) realization you are not truly the things you've identified with, and the "ego" or sense of self you've created in your mind is a fabrication
- Ketamine: A general anesthetic administered intravenously and intramuscularly in the form of its hydrochloride and used illicitly usually by being inhaled in powdered form especially for the dreamlike or hallucinogenic state it produces
- Neuroplasticity: Capacity of neurons and neural networks in the brain to change their connections and behavior in response to new information, sensory stimulation, development, damage, or dysfunction
- Psychedelics: Of, relating to, or being drugs (such as LSD) capable of producing abnormal psychic effects (such as hallucinations) and sometimes psychotic states

MENTAL FOOD FOR MODEL THOUGHTS

- Cassandra: A daughter of Priam endowed with the gift of prophecy but fated never to be believed

CLIMATE THOUGHTS & PATTERNS

- Echidna: A spiny-coated toothless burrowing nocturnal monotreme mammal (*Tachyglossus aculeatus*) of Australia,

Tasmania, and New Guinea that has a long extensible tongue and long heavy claws and feeds chiefly on ants
- Gestation crate: A metal enclosure in which a farmed sow used for breeding may be kept during pregnancy
- Humanewashing: The practice of making a misleading claim about the treatment of animals or the conditions in which they are born, raised, or killed

Appendix

EPIGRAPH

Alsbrooks, Billy. "Blessed and Unstoppable Quotes." Goodreads. Accessed March 1, 2022. https://www.goodreads.com/quotes/tag/blessed-and-unstoppable.

THE JOURNEY

IPCC. "Climate Change Widespread, Rapid, and Intensifying—IPCC." IPCC, August 9, 2021. https://www.ipcc.ch/2021/08/09/ar6-wg1-20210809-pr/.

Ivanova, Irina. "People Are Quitting Their Jobs at Record Rates. That's a Good Thing for the Economy." *CBS News*, June 21, 2021. https://www.cbsnews.com/news/workers-quitting-jobs-record-rate-economy/.

Kelly, Jack. "More Than Half of US Workers Are Unhappy in Their Jobs: Here's Why What Needs to Be Done Now." *Forbes*, October 25, 2019. https://www.forbes.com/sites/jackkelly/2019/10/25/

more-than-half-of-us-workers-are-unhappy-in-their-jobs-her-es-why-and-what-needs-to-be-done-now/?sh=4952a1b32024.

Krulwich, Robert. "You (And Almost Everyone You Know) Owe Your Life to This Man." *National Geographic*, March 24, 2016. https://www.nationalgeographic.com/culture/article/you-and-almost-everyone-you-know-owe-your-life-to-this-man.

Roth, Sammy. "Coal Plants Are Closing across the West. Here Are the Companies Sticking with Coal." *Los Angeles Times*, February 4, 2020. https://www.latimes.com/environment/story/2020-02-04/coal-power-plants-western-us.

Sönnichsen, N. "Coal Power Stations in the US by State 2021." Statista, October 7, 2021. https://www.statista.com/statistics/1252352/us-coal-power-plants-by-state/.

Thompson, Cheryl. "Fatal Police Shootings of Unarmed Black People Reveal Troubling Patterns." NPR, January 25, 2021. https://www.npr.org/2021/01/25/956177021/fatal-police-shootings-of-unarmed-black-people-reveal-troubling-patterns.

Vonnegut, Kurt. "Mother Night." Accessed March 1, 2022. https://www.shmoop.com/quotes/we-are-what-we-pretend-to-be.html.

Whitaker, Bill. "The Great Resignation: Why More Americans Are Quitting Their Jobs than Ever Before." *60 Minutes*. CBS News, January 9, 2022. https://www.cbsnews.com/news/great-resignation-60-minutes-2022-01-10/.

WHAT'S A MENTAL MODEL?

Abrams, Abigail. "Here's What We Know So Far about Russia's 2016 Meddling." *Time News*, April 18, 2019. https://time.com/5565991/russia-influence-2016-election/.

Bump, Philip. "What Trump Did about Coronavirus in February." *Washington Post*, April 20, 2020. https://www.washingtonpost.com/politics/2020/04/20/what-trump-did-about-coronavirus-february/.

Cadwalladr, Carole. "Revealed: 50 Million Facebook Profiles Harvested for Cambridge Analytica in Major Data Breach." *The Guardian*, March 17, 2018. https://www.theguardian.com/news/2018/mar/17/cambridge-analytica-facebook-influence-us-election.

CDC. "CDC Calls on Americans to Wear Masks to Prevent COVID-19 Spread." July 14, 2020. https://www.cdc.gov/media/releases/2020/p0714-americans-to-wear-masks.html.

Confessore, Nicholas. "Cambridge Analytica and Facebook: The Scandal and the Fallout So Far." *The New York Times*, April 4, 2018. https://www.nytimes.com/2018/04/04/us/politics/cambridge-analytica-scandal-fallout.html.

Eyal, Nir. 2014. *Hooked: How to Build Habit-Forming Products*. New York: Portfolio/Penguin.

Hoffa, James P. "James P. Hoffa Quotes." BrainyQuote.com. Accessed March 1, 2022. https://www.brainyquote.com/quotes/james_p_hoffa_416258.

Hozier. "Hozier Quotes." BrainyQuote.com. Accessed February 3, 2022. https://www.brainyquote.com/quotes/hozier_825693.

Mac, Ryan. "How Facebook Failed to Stem Racist Abuse of England's Soccer Players." *New York Times*, August 11, 2021. https://www.nytimes.com/2021/08/11/technology/facebook-soccer-racism.html.

Mencken, H. L. "H. L. Mencken Quotes." BrainyQuote.com. Accessed January 5, 2022. https://www.brainyquote.com/quotes/h_l_mencken_161245.

McKelvey, Tara. "Coronavirus: Why Are Americans So Angry about Masks?" BBC News, July 20, 2020. https://www.bbc.com/news/world-us-canada-53477121.

Pfizer. "Pfizer and BioNTech Announce Vaccine Candidate against COVID-19 Achieved Success in First Interim Analysis from Phase 3 Study." November 9, 2020. https://www.pfizer.com/news/press-release/press-release-detail/pfizer-and-biontech-announce-vaccine-candidate-against.

Roeder, Amy. "Social Media Use Can Be Positive for Mental Health and Well-Being." Harvard School of Public Health, January 6, 2020. https://www.hsph.harvard.edu/news/features/social-media-positive-mental-health/.

Rogers, Kaleigh. "Why Did the World Shut Down for COVID-19 but Not Ebola, Sars or Swine Flu?" FiveThirtyEight, April 14, 2020. https://fivethirtyeight.com/features/why-did-the-world-shut-down-for-covid-19-but-not-ebola-sars-or-swine-flu/.

Rotten Tomatoes. "*They Live* Quotes." Rotten Tomatoes.com. Accessed Jan 2, 2022. https://www.rottentomatoes.com/m/they_live/quotes/.

Ryan, Hana. "Who Wears a Mask and Why? Here's What the Data Say—And What We Should Do about It | Commentary." *The Baltimore Sun*, November 5, 2020. https://www.baltimoresun.com/opinion/op-ed/bs-ed-op-1108-mask-wearers-ryan-20201105-da6rnhuv7jccfhcx5wfc5vdkfi-story.html.

Senge, Peter. 1990. *The Fifth Discipline: The Art and Practice of the Learning Organization*. New York: Currency.

Sloan, Robin. *Mr. Penumbra's 24-Hour Bookstore*. Quoteslyfe.com. Accessed December 20, 2021. https://www.quoteslyfe.com/quote/All-the-secrets-of-the-world-worth-212134.

BENEFITS & SIDE EFFECTS

Angelou, Maya. "300 Maya Angelou Quotes." WisdomQuotes.com. Accessed February 14, 2022. https://wisdomquotes.com/maya-angelou-quotes/.

Battersby, Stephen. "The Impossible Barber and Other Bizarre Thought Experiments." *New Scientist*, May 11, 2016. https://www.newscientist.com/article/2087688-the-impossible-barber-and-other-bizarre-thought-experiments/.

Baum-Baicker. "The Psychological Benefits of Moderate Alcohol Consumption: A Review of the Literature." PubMed.gov, August 15, 1985. https://pubmed.ncbi.nlm.nih.gov/4053968/.

Bethel, Bill. "Bill Bethel Quotes." FinestQuotes.com. Accessed January 12, 2022. http://www.finestquotes.com/author_quotes-author-Bill+Bethel-page-0.htm.

Deutsch, Claudia. "At Kodak, Some Old Things Are New Again." *New York Times*, May 2, 2008. https://www.nytimes.com/2008/05/02/technology/02kodak.html.

Einstein, Albert. "Albert Einstein Quotes." BrainyQuote.com. Accessed November 14, 2021. https://www.brainyquote.com/quotes/albert_einstein_121993.

Farnam Street Media. "Mental Models: The Best Way to Make Intelligent Decisions (~100 Models Explained)." https://fs.blog/mental-models/#what_are_mental_models.

Goff-Dupont, Sarah. "How to Boost Your Team's Success with Shared Mental Models." *Atlassian*, December 21, 2020. https://www.atlassian.com/blog/teamwork/shared-mental-models-improve-team-performance.

Handwerk, Brian. "How Dexterous Thumbs May Have Helped Shape Evolution Two Million Years Ago." *Smithsonian Magazine*, January 28, 2021. https://www.smithsonianmag.com/science-nature/how-dexterous-thumbs-may-have-helped-shape-evolution-two-million-years-ago-180976870/.

Hale, Kori. "AI Bias Caused 80 Percent of Black Mortgage Applicants to Be Denied." *Forbes*, September 2, 2021. https://www.forbes.com/sites/korihale/2021/09/02/ai-bias-caused-80-of-black-mortgage-applicants-to-be-denied/?sh=4d33544f36fe.

Hanna, Ria. "Ria Hanna's Answer to 'as a Nurse, Have the Doctors Ever Treated You like an Inferior Part of the Patient's Care Team?'" Quora, January 7, 2020. https://www.quora.com/As-a-nurse-have-the-doctors-ever-treated-you-like-an-inferior-part-of-the-patient-s-care-team.

Kincaid, Andrew. "Heikegani—the Samurai Crab." Japan Powered, March 30, 2013. https://www.japanpowered.com/folklore-and-urban-legends/heikegani-the-samurai-crab.

Mack, Alexandra. 2010. *Spiritual Journey, Imperial City: Pilgrimage to the Temples of Vijayanagara*. New Delhi: Vedams.

Mattson, Mark. "Superior Pattern Processing Is the Essence of the Evolved Human Brain." National Center for Biotechnology Information, August 24, 2014. https://www.ncbi.nlm.nih.gov/pmc/articles/PMC4141622/.

Müller, Rebecca. "Effects of ICT Shared Mental Models on Team Processes and Outcomes." *SAGE Journals*, March 1, 2021. https://journals.sagepub.com/doi/abs/10.1177/1046496421997889.

Pallardy, Richard. "Chile Mine Rescue of 2010." *Britannica*, November 22, 2010. https://www.britannica.com/event/Chile-mine-rescue-of-2010.

Philips, Tony. "Unmasking the Face on Mars." NASA Science, May 23, 2001. https://science.nasa.gov/science-news/science-at-nasa/2001/ast24may_1.

Project Heartbeat. "ACLS Training Improves Team Response to Cardiac Arrest." Project Heartbeat, May 16, 2018. https://projectheartbeat.com/acls-training-improves-team-response/.

Robbins, Alexandra. "Doctors Throwing Fits." *Slate News*, April 29, 2015. https://slate.com/technology/2015/04/doctors-bully-nurses-hospital-mistreatment-is-a-danger-to-patient-health.html.

Satell, Greg. "A Look Back at Why Blockbuster Really Failed and Why It Didn't Have To." *Forbes*, September 5, 2014. https://www.forbes.com/sites/gregsatell/2014/09/05/a-look-back-at-why-blockbuster-really-failed-and-why-it-didnt-have-to/?sh=71052240id64.

Silver, David. "AlphaZero: Shedding New Light on Chess, Shogi, and Go." *DeepMind*, December 6, 2018. https://deepmind.com/blog/article/alphazero-shedding-new-light-grand-games-chess-shogi-and-go.

Sloane, Paul. "Are You Open Minded? Three Ways to Break Thinking Patterns | Paul Sloane | TEDxUniversityofBrighton." *YouTube*, uploaded by TEDX Talks, April 19, 2016. https://www.youtube.com/watch?v=4vgl3v8rjj8&ab_channel=TEDxTalks.

Tesla, Nikola. 1919. *My Inventions: The Autobiography of Nikola Tesla*. Eastford, CT: Experimenter Publishing Company, Inc.

Tishmack, Jody. "Our Opposable Thumb." Resilience, October 11, 2018. https://www.resilience.org/stories/2018-10-11/our-opposable-thumb/.

UNWTO. "Tourism Can Protect and Promote Religious Heritage." UNWTO, December 10, 2014. https://www.unwto.org/archive/europe/press-release/2014-12-10/tourism-can-protect-and-promote-religious-heritage.

Usborne, David. "The Moment It All Went Wrong for Kodak." *The Independent*, January 20, 2012. https://www.independent.co.uk/news/business/analysis-and-features/the-moment-it-all-went-wrong-for-kodak-6292212.html.

Vincent, James. "Twitter's Photo-Cropping Algorithm Prefers Young, Beautiful, and Light-Skinned Faces." *The Verge*, August 10, 2021. https://www.theverge.com/2021/8/10/22617972/twitter-photo-cropping-algorithm-ai-bias-bug-bounty-results.

Yen, John, Xiaocong Fan, Shuang Sun, Rui Wang, Cong Chen, and Kaivan Kamali. "Implementing Shared Mental Models for Collaborative Teamwork." CiteSeer, 2003. http://citeseerx.ist.psu.edu/viewdoc/summary?doi=10.1.1.61.2548.

TO CHANGE OR NOT TO CHANGE?

Chávez, Andrés. "Racial Problems in Ecuador." *INNOVA Research Journal*, October 2017. https://repositorio.uide.edu.ec/bitstream/37000/3768/15/%E2%80%9CProblemas%20Raciales%20en%20Ecuador%E2%80%9D.pdf.

Eckert, Eileen. "Invisible Force: Farmers' Mental Models and How They Influence Learning and Actions." *Journal of Extension*, June 2005. https://extension.unh.edu/adultlearning/invisibleforce.pdf.

Jensen, Christopher. "Anton Yelchin's Death Highlights a Known Issue with Jeeps." *New York Times*, June 21, 2016. https://www.nytimes.com/2016/06/22/business/anton-yelchins-death-highlights-a-known-issue-with-jeeps.html.

McGreal, Chris. "How America's Food Giants Swallowed the Family Farms." *The Guardian*, March 9, 2019. https://www.theguardian.com/environment/2019/mar/09/american-food-giants-swallow-the-family-farms-iowa.

Meyer, Zlati. "One-Third of Small Independent Farms Could Go Bankrupt in 2020 Due to COVID-19." *Fast Company*, June 1, 2020. https://www.fastcompany.com/90510325/one-third-of-small-independent-farms-could-go-bankrupt-in-2020-due-to-covid-19.

Noah, Trevor. "Exclusive—Tomi Lahren Extended Interview." *The Daily Show with Trevor Noah*. Comedy Central, November 30, 2016. https://www.cc.com/video/m9ds7s/the-daily-show-with-trevor-noah-exclusive-tomi-lahren-extended-interview?xrs=synd_twitter_120116_cc_tds_28&fbclid=IwAR2ek34aeKnDtGyYoWeguS3twIgArvw7yItGt7Ii8l-lolLkxPw3TA8UUm1M.

Norman, Donald. 1988. *The Design of Everyday Things*. New York: Basic Books.

Obasogie, Osagie. "A Q&A with Osagie K. Obasogie." *Stanford University Press Blog*, February 2014. https://stanfordpress.typepad.com/blog/2014/02/a-qa-with-osagie-k-obasogie.html.

Ramey, Jay. "FCA to Recall 1.1 Million Vehicles for Confusing Shifter." *Autoweek*, April 27, 2016. https://www.autoweek.com/news/a1844856/fca-recall-11-million-vehicles-confusing-shifter/.

Semuels, Alana. "'They're Trying to Wipe Us Off the Map.' Small American Farmers Are Nearing Extinction." *Time News*, November 20, 2019. https://time.com/5736789/small-american-farmers-debt-crisis-extinction/.

The Verge. "Why Chrysler's recalled gear shift is so bad." *YouTube*, uploaded by The Verge, June 26, 2016. https://www.youtube.com/watch?v=EQdnsrkjo6o&ab_channel=TheVerge.

Videlock, Wendy. "Change." Poetry Foundation, January 2009. https://www.poetryfoundation.org/poetrymagazine/poems/52001/change-56d2302224408.

World Population Review. "Ecuador Population 2021 (Live)." World Population Review, 2021. https://worldpopulationreview.com/countries/ecuador-population.

WHY APPLY

Badrinathan, Sumitra, Devesh Kapur, Jonathan Kay, and Milan Vaishnav. "Social Realities of Indian Americans: Results From the 2020 Indian American Attitudes Survey." Carnegie Endowment for International Peace, June 9, 2021. https://carnegieendowment.org/2021/06/09/social-realities-of-indian-americans-results-from-2020-indian-american-attitudes-survey-pub-84667.

Becker, Karen. "Individual and Organizational Unlearning: Directions for Future Research." *International Journal of Organizational Behavior*, 2005. https://www.researchgate.net/publication/27470611_Individual_and_organisational_unlearning_directions_for_future_research.

Bhuvanmohanan. YourQuote. Accessed January 11, 2022. https://www.yourquote.in/poovendhiran-mohanan-ie3/quotes/all-stuck-this-loop-called-life-doing-same-thing-over-again-hcd6t.

Boden, William, Robert A. O'Rourke, Koon K. Teo, Pamela M. Hartigan, David J. Maron, William J. Kostuk, Merril Knudtson, Marcin Dada, Paul Casperson, Crystal L. Harris, et al. "Optimal Medical Therapy with or without PCI for Stable Coronary Disease." PubMed, April 2007. https://pubmed.ncbi.nlm.nih.gov/17387127/.

Buchbinder, Rachelle et al. "A Randomized Trial of Vertebroplasty for Painful Osteoporotic Vertebral Fractures." PubMed, August 2009. https://pubmed.ncbi.nlm.nih.gov/19657121/.

Gupta, Divya et al. "The Physician's Experience of Changing Clinical Practice: A Struggle to Unlearn." Implementation Science, February 28, 2017. https://implementationscience.biomedcentral.com/articles/10.1186/s13012-017-0555-2.

HealthIT.gov. "Office-based Physician Electronic Health Record Adoption." HealthIT.gov, 2017. https://www.healthit.gov/data/quickstats/office-based-physician-electronic-health-record-adoption.

Howley, Elaine. "15 Ways to Shift Your Mindset for Better Weight Loss." US News, May 21, 2021. https://health.usnews.com/wellness/slideshows/ways-to-shift-your-mindset-for-better-weight-loss?slide=12.

Kahneman, Daniel. 2011. *Thinking, Fast and Slow.* New York: Farrar, Straus and Giroux.

Kerns, Sabrina. "Growing up Racist: Man Looks to Bring Change After Past." US News, June 20, 2020. https://www.usnews.com/news/best-states/georgia/articles/2020-06-20/growing-up-racist-man-looks-to-bring-change-after-past.

Krishnan, Vidya. "The Casteism I See in America." *The Atlantic*, November 6, 2021. https://www.theatlantic.com/ideas/archive/2021/11/india-america-caste/620583/.

Peck, M. Scott. AZQuotes.com. Accessed January 5, 2022. https://www.azquotes.com/quote/349919.

McNulty, Rose. "HRT Associated with Higher Breast Cancer Risk, Study Finds." *AJMC*, November 13, 2020. https://www.ajmc.com/view/hrt-associated-with-higher-breast-cancer-risk.

Miller, S H. "Unlearn." Hello Poetry, June 2013. Accessed February 24, 2022. https://hellopoetry.com/words/unlearn/.

Niven, Daniel. "Closing the 17-Year Gap between Scientific Evidence and Patient Care." University Affairs, January 17, 2017. https://www.universityaffairs.ca/opinion/in-my-opinion/closing-17-year-gap-scientific-evidence-patient-care/.

NPR. "California Workplace Discrimination System Sheds Light on Caste System." NPR, October 12, 2020. https://www.npr.org/2020/10/12/922936053/california-workplace-discrimination-system-sheds-light-on-caste-system.

Ray, Tinku. "The US Isn't Safe from the Trauma of Caste Bias." The World, March 8, 2019. https://theworld.org/stories/2019-03-08/us-isn-t-safe-trauma-caste-bias.

Rosenberg, Alan, Abiy Agiro, Marc Gottlieb, John Barron, Peter Brady, Ying Liu, Cindy Li, and Andrea DeVries. "Early Trends among Seven Recommendations from the Choosing Wisely Campaign." PubMed, December 2015. https://pubmed.ncbi.nlm.nih.gov/26457643/.

Sapolsky, Robert M. 2017. *Behave: The Biology of Humans at Our Best and Worst*. New York: Penguin Books.

ScienceDaily. "Faces of Black Children as Young as Five Evoke Negative Biases." ScienceDaily, February 8, 2016. www.sciencedaily.com/releases/2016/02/160208083140.htm.

Segal, Steven. 2004. *Business Feel: From the Science of Management to the Philosophy of Leadership*. London: Springer.

SmarterEveryDay. "The Backwards Brain Bicycle—Smarter Every Day 133." *YouTube*, uploaded by SmarterEveryDay, April 24, 2015. https://www.youtube.com/watch?v=MFzDaBzBlLo&ab_channel=SmarterEveryDay.

Stringfellow, Erin. "'You Have to Want It': A Pervasive Mental Model of Addiction Recovery and Its Implications for Sustaining Change." Washington University Open Scholarship, May 15, 2019. https://openscholarship.wustl.edu/cgi/viewcontent. cgi?article=2792&context=art_sci_etds.

WebMD. "Hormone Replacement Therapy and Breast Cancer Risk." WebMD, August 25, 2020. https://www.webmd.com/ breast-cancer/breast-cancer-hormone-replacement-therapy-cancer-risk.

Wilkerson, Isabel. "America's 'Untouchables': The Silent Power of the Caste System." *The Guardian*, July 28, 2020. https://www. theguardian.com/world/2020/jul/28/untouchables-caste-system-us-race-martin-luther-king-india.

Wilkerson, Isabel. 2020. *Caste: The Origins of Our Discontents*. New York: Random House.

Zeal 4 Knowledge. "Manly P Hall: How to Master Your Thinking Patterns and Habits for Self-Development Wisdom Lecture." *YouTube*, uploaded by Zeal 4 Knowledge, June 22, 2019. https:// www.youtube.com/watch?v=KvZ7CRGRJtE&ab_channel=Zeal4Knowledge.

SUPERPOWERS

Beek, Sophia. "Substance Abuse in the COVID Era." Tower Masters NY, January 6, 2021. https://tower.mastersny.org/6691/ features/subsance-abuse-in-the-covid-era/.

Brown, Brene. "Lotus Pathway." Pinterest. https://www.pinterest. com/pin/authenticity-is-the-daily-practice-of-letting-go-who-we-think-were-supposed-to-be-and-embracing-who-we-are--625718941956050442/.

Dean, Grace. "Nearly Three-Quarters of Workers Are Actively Thinking About Quitting Their Job, According to a Recent Survey." *Business Insider*, October 7, 2021. https://www.businessinsider.com/great-resignation-labor-shortage-workers-thinking-about-quitting-joblist-report-2021-10.

Dictionary.com. "Dissociate." https://www.dictionary.com/browse/dissociate.

Eurich, Tasha. "The Right Way to Be Introspective (Yes, There's a Wrong Way)." Ideas.Ted.com, June 2, 2017. https://ideas.ted.com/the-right-way-to-be-introspective-yes-theres-a-wrong-way/.

Hagen, Nina. "Superpowers Quotes." BrainyQuote. Accessed February 4, 2022. https://www.brainyquote.com/quotes/nina_hagen_765843?src=t_superpowers.

Heltzel, Gordon, and Kristin Laurin. "Polarization in America: Two Possible Futures." National Center for Biotechnology Information, May 6, 2020. https://www.ncbi.nlm.nih.gov/pmc/articles/PMC7201237/.

McAlinden, Mona. "'Lockdown Boredom Led Me to Smoke More Weed.'" BBC News, May 30, 2020. https://www.bbc.com/news/uk-scotland-52849794.

Nezlek, John B. "Day-To-Day Relationships between Self-Awareness, Daily Events, and Anxiety." Wiley Online Library, *Jour-*

nal of Personality, November 23, 2002. https://onlinelibrary. wiley.com/doi/abs/10.1111/1467-6494.05005.

Park, Julie J. and Melissa L. Millora. "The Relevance of Reflection: An Empirical Examination of the Role of Reflection in Ethic of Caring, Leadership, and Psychological Well-Being." Project MUSE, March 2012. https://muse.jhu.edu/article/469343/pdf.

Rotten Tomatoes. "Marvel Movies in Order: How to Watch All 27 MCU Movies." https://editorial.rottentomatoes.com/guide/marvel-movies-in-order/.

Sherlock, Ben. "10 Most Impressive Box Office Records Broken by the MCU." Screen Rant, May 5, 2020. https://screenrant.com/mcu-most-impressive-box-office-records-broken/.

Smith, Morgan. "Professor Who Predicted 'the Great Resignation' Shares the 3 Trends That Will Dominate Work in 2022." *Make It*. CNBC, January 14, 2022. https://www.cnbc.com/2022/01/14/the-great-resignation-expert-shares-the-biggest-work-trends-of-2022.html.

Stein D, Grant. "Disentangling the Relationships among Self-Reflection, Insight, and Subjective Well-Being: The Role of Dysfunctional Attitudes and Core Self-Evaluations." PubMed.gov, September 2014. https://pubmed.ncbi.nlm.nih.gov/25087316/.

Tugaleva, Vironika. "Disagreement Quotes." Goodreads. Accessed February 15, 2022. https://www.goodreads.com/quotes/tag/disagreements.

Woodcock, Naomi. "A Superhero." CityWise, July 2019. https://citywise.org/a-superhero-poem/.

Zagorsky, Jay. "The Great Resignation: Data and Analysis Show It's Not as Great as Screaming Headlines Suggest." *The Nevada Current*, January 14, 2022. https://www.nevadacurrent.com/2022/01/14/the-great-resignation-data-and-analysis-show-its-not-as-great-as-screaming-headlines-suggest/.

ALTER, DON'T FALTER

ACT Auntie. Accessed February 24, 2022. https://m.facebook.com/ABCTnow/photos/a.547877568606109/2367146350012546/?type=3&source=57.

Asimov, Isaac. 1957. *The Naked Sun*. New York: Doubleday https://www.goodreads.com/work/quotes/1583154-the-naked-sun.

Bell, Leigh. "Health Insurance Coverage for Binge Eating Disorder." EatingDisorderHope.com, September 18, 2015. https://www.eatingdisorderhope.com/insurance-coverage-binge-eating-disorder.

Corliss, Julie. "Mindfulness Meditation May Ease Anxiety, Mental Stress." *Harvard Health Blog*, January 8, 2014. https://www.health.harvard.edu/blog/mindfulness-meditation-may-ease-anxiety-mental-stress-201401086967.

de Vos, Cato M H et al. "Psychedelics and Neuroplasticity: A Systematic Review Unraveling the Biological Underpinnings of Psychedelics." National Center for Biotechnology Information, September 10, 2021. https://www.ncbi.nlm.nih.gov/pmc/articles/PMC8461007/.

Dolan, Eric. "Neuroscience Study Finds Evidence That Meditation Increases the Entropy of Brainwaves." PsyPost, February 11, 2020. https://www.psypost.org/2020/02/neuroscience-study-finds-evidence-that-meditation-increases-the-entropy-of-brainwaves-55513.

Ghazavi, Zahra, Esmat Rahimi, Mohsen Yazdani, Hamid Afshar et al. "Effect of Cognitive Behavioral Stress Management Program on Psychosomatic Patients' Quality of Life." National Center for Biotechnology Information, September 2016. https://www.ncbi.nlm.nih.gov/pmc/articles/PMC5114797/.

Hall, Wayne. "Why Was Early Therapeutic Research on Psychedelic Drugs Abandoned?" *Psychological Medicine*. Cambridge University Press, October 21, 2021. https://www.cambridge.org/core/journals/psychological-medicine/article/abs/why-was-early-therapeutic-research-on-psychedelic-drugs-abandoned/59F93D11DE21F420465559BBEB99CC14.

Hopwood, Tanya and Nicola Schutte. "A Meta-Analytic Investigation of the Impact of Mindfulness-Based Interventions on Post Traumatic Stress." *ScienceDirect Clinical Psychology Review*, Vol. 57. November 2017. https://www.sciencedirect.com/science/article/abs/pii/S0272735817301551?via%3Dihub.

Kabat-Zinn, Jon. 1994. *Wherever You Go, There You Are*. New York: Hachette Books.

Kaczkurkin, Antonia N., and Edna B. Foa. "Cognitive-Behavioral Therapy for Anxiety Disorders: An Update on the Empirical Evidence." National Center for Biotechnology Information, September 2015. https://www.ncbi.nlm.nih.gov/pmc/articles/PMC4610618/.

LaRosa, John. "$1.2 Billion U.S. Meditation Market Growing Strongly as It Becomes More Mainstream." *Market Research Blog*, October 16, 2019. https://blog.marketresearch.com/1.2-billion-u.s.-meditation-market-growing-strongly-as-it-becomes-more-mainstream.

Lenehan, Arthur. 1994. *The Best of Bits & Pieces*. Fairfield, NJ: Economics Press.

Marquez, RJ. "Research Shows Meditation Has Power Effects on the Brain." *KSAT News*, January 9, 2022. https://www.ksat.com/news/local/2022/01/09/research-shows-meditation-has-power-effects-on-the-brain/.

McKenna, Terence. "Psychedelic Quotes." Goodreads. Accessed January 4, 2022. https://www.goodreads.com/quotes/tag/psychedelics.

Millière, Raphaël et al. "Psychedelics, Meditation, and Self-Consciousness." *Frontiers in Psychology*, September 4, 2018. https://www.frontiersin.org/articles/10.3389/fpsyg.2018.01475/full.

Murphy, Rebecca et al. "Cognitive Behavioral Therapy for Eating Disorders." National Center for Biotechnology Information, September 2010. https://www.ncbi.nlm.nih.gov/pmc/articles/PMC2928448/.

O'Neill, Stephanie. "A New Way to Quit? Psychedelic Therapy Offers Promise for Smoking Cessation." NPR, December 22, 2019. https://www.npr.org/sections/health-shots/2019/12/22/774385634/a-new-way-to-quit-psychedelic-therapy-offers-promise-for-smoking-cessation.

Pajer, Nicole. "Quiet the Mind and Get Your Zen on with These 50 Quotes About Meditation." *Parade*, November 1, 2021. https://parade.com/1066461/nicolepajer/meditation-quotes/.

Perry, Kevin. "Are Psychedelic Drugs the Answer to Veterans' PTSD?" *Men's Health*, September 24, 2021. https://www.menshealth.com/uk/mental-strength/a36488173/psychedelic-drug-ayahuasca-veterans-ptsd/.

Rumi, Jalaluddin. "The Guest House." Scottish Poetry Library, https://www.scottishpoetrylibrary.org.uk/poem/guest-house/.

Senthilingam, Meera. "Can Meditation and Psychedelics Have the Same Benefits for Your Mind?" CNN Health, June 3, 2016. https://www.cnn.com/2016/06/03/health/psychedelics-anxiety-depression-meditation/index.html.

Slater, Lauren. "How Psychedelic Drugs Can Help Patients Face Death." *New York Times*, April 20, 2012. https://www.nytimes.com/2012/04/22/magazine/how-psychedelic-drugs-can-help-patients-face-death.html.

Stieg, Cory. "Psychedelic Trips Could Soon Be Part of Therapy—Here's What Those Sessions Will Look Like." CNBC, July 24, 2021. https://www-cnbc-com.cdn.ampproject.org/c/s/www.

cnbc.com/amp/2021/07/24/how-psychedelic-assisted-thera-py-with-mdma-and-psilocybin-works.html.

Tang, Qing-Lin, Guo-Yao Lin, and Ming-Qing Zhang. "Cognitive-behavioral Therapy for the Management of Irritable Bowel Syndrome." National Center for Biotechnology Information, December 14, 2013. https://www.ncbi.nlm.nih.gov/pmc/articles/PMC3870505/.

Tatala, Dorien. "Every Psychedelic Study Currently Going on in Europe." Interdisciplinary Conference on Psychedelic Research, August 25, 2020. https://icpr2020.net/europes-psychedelic-science-renaissance/.

Transcendental Meditation. "Transcendental Meditation Turns 60." PR Newswire, July 9, 2019. https://www.prnewswire.com/news-releases/transcendental-meditation-turns-60-300881154.html.

Wiginton, Keri. "Nothing Worked for My Depression—Until I Tried Meditation." *The Washington Post*, February 26, 2018. https://www.washingtonpost.com/news/inspired-life/wp/2018/02/26/nothing-worked-for-my-depression-until-i-tried-meditation/.

Wilson, Clare. "Mindfulness and Meditation Can Worsen Depression and Anxiety." *New Scientist*, August 14, 2020. https://www.newscientist.com/article/2251840-mindfulness-and-meditation-can-worsen-depression-and-anxiety/.

Zulkey, Claire. "How Therapy Can Cure Overeating." *The Atlantic*, August 23, 2017. https://www.theatlantic.com/health/archive/2017/08/how-therapy-can-cure-overeating/537537/.

MENTAL FOOD FOR MODEL THOUGHTS

Afiyah the Poet. "Loop." Medium, October 4, 2020. https://medium.com/scribe/loop-139b3d6dcb00.

Movieclips. "Blue Pill or Red Pill—*The Matrix* (2/9) Movie Clip (1999) HD." YouTube, uploaded by Movieclips, May 26, 2011. https://www.youtube.com/watch?v=EQdnsrkjo6o&ab_channel=TheVerge.

CLIMATE THOUGHTS & PATTERNS

Bain, Paul, Esmat Rahimi, Mohsen Yazdani, and Hamid Afshar, Taciano L. Milfont, Yoshihisa Kashima, Michał Bilewicz, et al. "Co-benefits of Addressing Climate Change Can Motivate Action Around the World." *Nature*, September 28, 2015. https://www.nature.com/articles/nclimate2814.

Bokat-Lindell, Spencer. "So You Want to Convince a Climate Change Skeptic." *New York Times*, January 2, 2020. https://www.nytimes.com/2020/01/02/opinion/climate-change-deniers.html.

Congressional Research Service. "Greenhouse Gas Emissions and Sinks in US Agriculture." Sgp.fas.org, September 2, 2021. https://sgp.fas.org/crs/misc/IF11404.pdf.

C.O.nxt. "Food Label Claims That Make Consumers More Likely to Buy." *C.O.nxt.* https://co-nxt.com/blog/food-label-claims-that-make-consumers-more-likely-to-buy/.

Lawson, Danielle, Kathryn T. Stevenson, M. Nils Peterson, Sarah J. Carrier, Renee L. Strnad, and Erin Seekamp. "Children Can Foster Climate Change Concern Among Their Parents." *Nature*, May 6, 2019. https://www.nature.com/articles/s41558-019-0463-3.

Loria, Kevin. "Cities Around the US Are Flooding at High Tide and on Sunny Days at Record Rates—Here's What It's Like." *Business Insider*, June 12, 2018. https://www.businessinsider.com/sea-level-rise-high-tides-sunny-day-flooding-coastal-cities-2018-4.

McKie, Robin. "Miami, the Great World City, Is Drowning While the Powers That Be Look Away." *The Guardian*, July 11, 2014. https://www.theguardian.com/world/2014/jul/11/miami-drowning-climate-change-deniers-sea-levels-rising.

Miller, Sarah. "Heaven or High Water." *Popula*, April 2, 2019. https://popula.com/2019/04/02/heaven-or-high-water/.

Milman, Oliver. "US Emissions Roared Back Last Year After Pandemic Drop, Figures Show." *The Guardian*, January 10, 2022. https://www.theguardian.com/environment/2022/jan/10/us-emissions-climate-crisis-global-heating.

Thunberg, Greta. "15 Greta Thunberg Quotes That'll Motivate You to Do Something About Climate Change." FairyGodBoss. Accessed February 24, 2022. https://fairygodboss.com/career-topics/greta-thunberg-quotes.

Wolsko, Christopher, Hector Ariceaga, and Jesse Seiden. "Red, White, and Blue Enough to Be Green: Effects of Moral Framing on Climate Change Attitudes and Conservation Behaviors." *Journal of Experimental Social Psychology*, Vol. 65. February 2016. https://www.researchgate.net/publication/295677478_Red_White_and_Blue_Enough_to_Be_Green_Effects_of_Moral_Framing_on_Climate_Change_Attitudes_and_Conservation_Behaviors.

GLOSSARY

Animal Legal Defense Fund. "How False Advertising Lawsuits Help Animals." https://aldf.org/article/how-false-advertising-lawsuits-help-animals/.

Britannica. s.v. "mestizo." Accessed February 7, 2022. https://www.britannica.com/topic/mestizo.

Britannica. s.v. "neuroplasticity." Accessed February 7, 2022. https://www.britannica.com/science/neuroplasticity.

Bhandari, Smitha. "What Is Dopamine?" WebMD, June 14, 2021. https://www.webmd.com/mental-health/what-is-dopamine.

Dictionary.com. s.v. "Ubermensch." Accessed February 7, 2022. https://www.vocabulary.com/dictionary/Ubermensch.

FirstPost.com. "Why Billionaire Carl Icahn's Is Feuding With McDonald's Over Gestation Crates." February 22, 2022. https://www.firstpost.com/world/why-billionaire-carl-icahns-is-feuding-with-mcdonalds-over-gestation-crates-10398861.html.

Foucault, Michel. *The History of Sexuality*, Vol. 1. Pantheon, 1978, p. 137.

Lexico. s.v. "platitude." Accessed February 7, 2022. https://www.lexico.com/en/definition/platitude.

Merriam-Webster.com. s.v. "adage." Accessed February 7, 2022. https://www.merriam-webster.com/dictionary/adage.

Merriam-Webster.com. s.v. "antagonism." Accessed February 7, 2022. https://www.merriam-webster.com/dictionary/antagonism.

Merriam-Webster.com. s.v. "apocryphal." Accessed February 7, 2022. https://www.merriam-webster.com/dictionary/apocryphal.

Merriam-Webster.com. s.v. "ayahuasca." Accessed February 7, 2022. https://www.merriam-webster.com/dictionary/ayahuasca.

Merriam-Webster.com. s.v. "balk." Accessed February 7, 2022. https://www.merriam-webster.com/dictionary/balk.

Merriam-Webster.com. s.v. "bulimia." Accessed February 7, 2022. https://www.merriam-webster.com/dictionary/bulimia.

Merriam-Webster.com. s.v. "cassandra." Accessed February 7, 2022. https://www.merriam-webster.com/dictionary/Cassandra.

Merriam-Webster.com. s.v. "caste." Accessed February 7, 2022. https://www.merriam-webster.com/dictionary/caste.

Merriam-Webster.com. s.v. "depth charge." Accessed February 7, 2022. https://www.merriam-webster.com/dictionary/depth%20charge.

Merriam-Webster.com. s.v. "echidna." Accessed February 7, 2022. https://www.merriam-webster.com/dictionary/echidna.

Merriam-Webster.com. s.v. "enjoin." Accessed February 7, 2022. https://www.merriam-webster.com/dictionary/enjoin.

Merriam-Webster.com. s.v. "eurocentric." Accessed February 7, 2022. https://www.merriam-webster.com/dictionary/Eurocentric.

Merriam-Webster.com. s.v. "incommunicado." Accessed February 7, 2022. https://www.merriam-webster.com/dictionary/incommunicado.

Merriam-Webster.com. s.v. "innocuous." Accessed February 7, 2022. https://www.merriam-webster.com/dictionary/innocuous

Merriam-Webster.com. s.v. "ketamine." Accessed February 7, 2022. https://www.merriam-webster.com/dictionary/ketamine

Merriam-Webster.com. s.v. "pareidolia." Accessed February 7, 2022. https://www.merriam-webster.com/dictionary/pareidolia.

Merriam-Webster.com. s.v. "precocious." Accessed February 7, 2022. https://www.merriam-webster.com/dictionary/precocious.

Merriam-Webster.com. s.v. "psychedelics." Accessed February 7, 2022. https://www.merriam-webster.com/dictionary/psychedelics.

Merriam-Webster.com. s.v. "transfix." Accessed February 7, 2022. https://www.merriam-webster.com/dictionary/transfix.

Merriam-Webster.com. s.v. "uighur." Accessed February 7, 2022. https://www.merriam-webster.com/dictionary/Uighur.

Merriam-Webster.com. s.v. "upend." Accessed February 7, 2022. https://www.merriam-webster.com/dictionary/upend.

Patowary, Kaushik. "Heikegani: The Crab with a Human Face." Amusing Planet, June 26, 2017. https://www.amusingplanet.com/2017/06/heikegani-crab-with-human-face.html.

Regan, Sarah. "Everything To Know About Ego Death—From What It Is to How It Happens." MBG Mindfulness, December 30, 2021. https://www.mindbodygreen.com/articles/ego-death.